At Issue

| Uranium Mining

DØ746242

Opening Day Collection

FRIENDS OF THE DAVIS PUBLIC LIBRARY

7,000 New Books

Other Books in the At Issue Series:

At Issue

Uranium Mining

Tamara Thompson, Book Editor

Yolo County Library
226 Buckeye Street
Woodland, CA 95695
530-666-8005

GREENHAVEN PRESS
A part of Gale, Cengage Learning

GALE
CENGAGE Learning™

Detroit • New York • San Francisco • New Haven, Conn • Waterville, Maine • London

Christine Nasso, *Publisher*
Elizabeth Des Chenes, *Managing Editor*

© 2011 Greenhaven Press, a part of Gale, Cengage Learning.

Gale and Greenhaven Press are registered trademarks used herein under license.

For more information, contact:
Greenhaven Press
27500 Drake Rd.
Farmington Hills, MI 48331-3535
Or you can visit our Internet site at gale.cengage.com

ALL RIGHTS RESERVED.
No part of this work covered by the copyright herein may be reproduced, transmitted, stored, or used in any form or by any means graphic, electronic, or mechanical, including but not limited to photocopying, recording, scanning, digitizing, taping, Web distribution, information networks, or information storage and retrieval systems, except as permitted under Section 107 or 108 of the 1976 United States Copyright Act, without the prior written permission of the publisher.

For product information and technology assistance, contact us at

Gale Customer Support, 1-800-877-4253
For permission to use material from this text or product, submit all requests online at
www.cengage.com/permissions

Further permissions questions can be e-mailed to permissionrequest@cengage.com

Articles in Greenhaven Press anthologies are often edited for length to meet page requirements. In addition, original titles of these works are changed to clearly present the main thesis and to explicitly indicate the author's opinion. Every effort is made to ensure that Greenhaven Press accurately reflects the original intent of the authors. Every effort has been made to trace the owners of copyrighted material.

Cover Image copyright © Images.com/Corbis.

LIBRARY OF CONGRESS CATALOGING-IN-PUBLICATION DATA

Uranium mining / Tamara Thompson, book editor.
p. cm. -- (At issue)
Includes bibliographical references and index.
ISBN 978-0-7377-4898-7 (hardcover) -- ISBN 978-0-7377-4899-4 (pbk.)
1. Uranium mines and mining--Environmental aspects--Popular works. 2. Uranium mines and mining--Economic aspects--Popular works. I. Thompson, Tamara.
TD195.U7U74 2010
338.2'74932--dc22

2010015278

Printed in the United States of America
1 2 3 4 5 6 7 14 13 12 11 10

Contents

Introduction

In the 2009 blockbuster movie, *Avatar*, a mining conglomerate sets its sights on a highly profitable, fictitious mineral called unobtanium, found only on a planet occupied by indigenous people called the Na'vi. The plot turns on the Na'vi's resistance to mining and the mining industry's greedy exploitation of the planet and its people. While the story is a phantasmagoric work of fiction, there are unsettling parallels to what actually happened to the Navajo in the American Southwest during the 30-year uranium boom that started in the 1950s—and what is happening now on uranium-rich indigenous lands worldwide.

The history of uranium mining is a troubling one, and the controversies surrounding the substance itself are many. Uranium is one of the rarest elements on the planet and is the heaviest metal in nature. It is also radioactive, which means it is highly unstable and comes apart at the atomic level—making it the perfect raw material for nuclear fission power. In the United States, uranium was initially mined in the 1950s to fuel the nuclear arms race between America and the Soviet Union during the Cold War. In the 1960s, it also became the fuel for power-generating nuclear reactors.

But before it can become fuel, uranium "yellowcake" must be extracted from the ground and processed to separate usable uranium from other rock substances and from its own toxic byproducts. When mined most commonly in open pits, ore is removed and then crushed and treated with chemicals to extract the uranium. This process generates huge piles of waste, known as "tailings," that are contaminated with radioactive byproducts, such as radium, thorium, and radon, as well as with toxic cyanide and various acids used to leach the uranium from the other materials.

In the American Southwest, more than 1,000 uranium mines on Navajo Nation land extracted thirteen million tons of uranium ore from 1945 to 1988, mostly employing tribe members as mine workers. Because they were unknowingly exposed to radioactive and toxic substances, many Navajo miners were stricken with cancers and other illnesses. Poor safety practices allowed radioactive dust to spread throughout communities, sickening miners' families and people who lived near the mines and poisoning the land and water for generations to come.

After the Navajos' plight was documented and publicized, Congress passed the Radiation Exposure Compensation Act in 1990 to pay some Navajo miners for their health problems; but not all miners qualified, and the Act did nothing to clean up contamination or help sick Navajos who did not work in the mines. When mining ended on Navajo lands in the late 1980s—due to growing public opposition to nuclear power and decreased demand for uranium as the Cold War ended— the radioactive mines and tailings piles were simply abandoned.

Over the years, open pit mines became rain-filled lakes and Navajos used them for drinking water and for their crops and animals. Children swam in the former mine pits and played in the sandy tailings. Seen as free building materials, tailings and large chunks of uranium ore were used to build many Navajo homes, unwittingly making them radioactive. Many Navajos still drink contaminated water, breathe radioactive dust, and live in radioactive homes today, and more than 1,000 abandoned uranium mines and tailing piles on Navajo Nation land have yet to be cleaned up. The sickness and death continue. Now, some fifty years after the contamination began, Congress is still holding hearings, trying to decide what to do about it.

"In this classic environmental justice story, we see how long native peoples have been burdened with inhumane levels of contamination, and we see how long it can take just to begin to undo the damage that the contamination brings," U.S. Representative Dennis Kucinich (D-Ohio) told a House of Representatives committee during a 2007 hearing on the health impacts of uranium mining on the Navajo Nation.

Although the Navajo legacy often takes center stage in discussions about uranium mining, it is a small part of the picture. The United States has less than 5 percent of the world's uranium supply. Australia, Canada, and Kazakhstan together account for 59 percent of the global reserves, and hence have more and bigger mines. Astonishingly, about 70 percent of the world's uranium deposits are on sovereign indigenous lands: ancestral Aboriginal lands in Australia, territories of the Inuit in Canada and the Navajo in the United States, and the lands of the nomadic Tuareg people in northern Niger, to name a few. The Navajo Nation today leads a vocal international movement to oppose uranium mining on native lands worldwide. Like the Na'vi of *Avatar*'s fictional planet Pandora, indigenous people on several continents are resisting heavy pressure to open up their sacred lands and expose their communities to the influences of industrial mining.

Meanwhile, the global demand for uranium keeps sky-rocketing, driven by a "nuclear renaissance" that views nuclear power as a pollution-free solution to global climate change. The renewed interest has jump-started uranium mine development globally and spurred a land rush in the American Southwest, where mining companies have staked thousands of new claims in hopes of cashing in on a second uranium boom. In 2005, the Navajo Nation voted to ban all uranium mining on its lands but is under continuing pressure to forgive the past and trust that new uranium extraction methods will be both safe and profitable for the tribe.

Mining industry officials say this time will be different because open pit mining has been replaced by in-situ leaching (ISL), a process in which miners pump liquids through holes drilled into uranium deposits and recover ore by leaching, rather than by breaking apart rock. While the industry heralds ISL as an advancement that makes uranium mining safe, critics argue that it poses an unacceptably high risk of contaminating water supplies if an accident or heavy rain releases some of the leach. As an example, they point to the 1979 disaster at Church Rock, New Mexico, in which 90 million gallons of liquid radioactive uranium mill waste reached the Rio Puerco River, which remains badly contaminated today.

Officials say such concerns are unfounded because the industry has changed so much over the past sixty years. They point out that in the United States there are now radiation protection standards to protect workers, pollutant discharge limits and drinking water standards to prevent groundwater contamination, and strict licensing and monitoring programs to regulate mining practices. Various government agencies enforce safety, health, and environmental standards to protect the public and the environment from the recognized dangers of uranium mining. Nevertheless, critics say that no matter how tempting the promise of clean nuclear power might be, ISL is not worth the risk because the consequences of water pollution are so devastating and long lasting.

Regardless, American public policy appears to be shifting back toward nuclear power solutions. In February 2010, President Barack Obama announced $8.3 billion in loans to help build the first U.S. nuclear power plants in nearly three decades, a move he said "is only the beginning" of an eventual $50 billion commitment to nuclear power. As the cornerstone of the nuclear fuel cycle, uranium mining will likely enjoy renewed favor over the coming decades, both in America and elsewhere. Whether the industry can make amends for its difficult history by becoming the sustainable energy answer to global climate change still remains to be seen. In his 2009 book, *Uranium: War, Energy and the Rock That Shaped the World*, Tom Zoellner sums it up this way: "The stability of our world rests on a substance that is unstable at the core. This is the fundamental paradox of uranium, the strongest element the earth can yield and one whose story is a fascinating window into the valor, greed, genius, and folly of humanity." The authors in *At Issue: Uranium Mining* represent a wide range of viewpoints concerning the benefits and consequences of uranium extraction—past, present and future.

1

The Benefits of Uranium Mining Outweigh Its Drawbacks

Jack Spencer and Nick Loris

Jack Spencer is research fellow in Nuclear Energy and Nicolas Loris is a research assistant, both at the Thomas A. Roe Institute for Economic Policy Studies at the Heritage Foundation, a conservative public policy research institute.

Uranium is an essential component of nuclear energy, and more uranium mines are needed to meet the growing global demand for nuclear power. Because nuclear energy is such a safe, cheap and clean source of power, the benefits of uranium mining far outweigh its drawbacks. Modern uranium mining is no more dangerous than other forms of mining, and companies who do it should not have to deal with unnecessary government oversight and regulations. The United States in particular should relax its opposition to uranium mining because it hinders the development of nuclear power, a badly needed source of clean and affordable energy.

Burdensome regulation, politics, and bad policy hamper access to available energy resources in the United States. The nation can now add uranium to the list of energy resources that local, state, and federal bureaucrats have deemed off-limits, which includes oil in the Arctic, off-shore natural gas, coastal wind, and cellulosic ethanol.

Jack Spencer and Nick Loris, "Uranium Mining Is Important for Securing America's Energy Future," *The Heritage Foundation Web Memo*, March 25, 2008. Copyright © 2008 The Heritage Foundation. Reproduced by permission.

The nation's largest known uranium deposit was discovered in the 1980s on a farm in southern Virginia. The owner of that land has recently explored the possibility of mining the approximately $10 billion worth of uranium believed to be on the site. Despite the fact that uranium has been mined safely around the world for decades, including in New Mexico, Nebraska, Utah, and Wyoming, Virginia bureaucrats have decided to prohibit land owners from even studying the viability of mining.

As the only proven power source that affordably provides large amounts of primarily domestic energy without atmospheric emissions, nuclear energy is a logical choice for a nation struggling to reconcile its energy policy with its economic, environmental, and security objectives. Like other large power generators, nuclear power plants need fuel. In the U.S., that fuel is uranium. As nuclear power expands, it will be critical that uranium resources are accessible when mining can be done in a safe and economical way.

Uranium: A Must-Have for Nuclear Power

To produce the same amount of electricity, nuclear power requires far less fuel than does coal, natural gas, petroleum and other energy sources. Still, some fuel is required.

Natural uranium is critical in the production of electricity through nuclear power.

Uranium is found throughout the world, but quantities sufficient to be mined economically are limited to a few known regions. Canada has the highest grade uranium while Australia has the most. Kazakhstan, South Africa, Niger, Namibia, and Brazil also have significant deposits. The U.S. has about 3 percent–4 percent of the world's known uranium and produces about 4.3 percent of the world's supply despite operating about one-quarter of the world's commercial power reactors.

Natural uranium is critical in the production of electricity through nuclear power. In its natural state, uranium consists of several isotopes. The isotope needed to conduct fission—the process that creates the heat necessary to produce power—is uranium-235 (U-235) and makes up 0.7 percent of naturally occurring uranium. The remainder is primarily uranium-238 (U-238).

However, for fission to be sustained in U.S. light water reactors, the uranium fuel must consist of approximately 3 percent–5 percent U-235. To reach this level, natural uranium must be enriched. Once the correct level of U-235 is attained, the uranium is manufactured into small pellets about the size of a pencil eraser. Each uranium pellet contains as much energy as 150 gallons of oil.

Increasing Demand for Uranium

Increasing production of nuclear power and higher production efficiency (which results in more fuel usage) inevitably mean a higher demand for uranium. Uranium production from mines eclipsed 39,000 tons in 2006. According to the World Nuclear Association, uranium requirements for fuel reactors could surpass 100,000 tons by 2020. Given that more than half of the world's uranium production comes from three countries, the U.S. faces substantial incentives to increase access to domestic uranium mining.

A nuclear renaissance is emerging worldwide. Countries like the United Kingdom, China, India, and Russia are planning significant expansions of nuclear energy; other nations are also planning new reactors. Indeed, some 35 reactors are under construction today throughout the world. U.S companies are planning to build up to 30 new reactors—though none have actually started construction.

Building all of these reactors would likely put substantial pressure on current uranium supplies. This is one reason why the United States must consider tapping more of its own uranium reserves. One place where that could happen is in Pittsylvania County, Virginia, where a 200-acre farm sits on an estimated 110 million pounds of uranium. This could fuel each of America's 104 nuclear reactors, which provide the U.S. with 20 percent of its electricity, for two years. Regrettably, Virginia banned uranium mining in 1982 and exhibits little inclination to reconsider this needless policy.

Energy Access Denied

Despite rising energy prices, government at all levels continues to deny Americans access to significant portions of the nation's energy resources. These legislative, bureaucratic, and procedural barriers are even more bizarre considering growing calls for energy independence. This affects uranium mining as well as Alaskan oil drilling, off-shore gas exploration, and wind farms.

Ironically, Virginia has a rich history of supporting nuclear power and continues to depend on it today. Its ban on uranium mining demonstrates the impact that anti-nuclear propaganda has had on the population. Virginia gets 38 percent of its electricity from four nuclear reactors and will likely be among the first to build a new reactor in the United States. Beyond that, Virginia hosts a variety of other nuclear-related industries, including the nuclear qualified Newport News naval shipyard, which is one of the nation's only two with that capability.

Virginia will surely not be the only place in the U.S. that attempts to prohibit access to uranium reserves as rising demand spurs exploration activities. Three decades of anti-nuclear propaganda continues to influence the public perception of nuclear power.

Mining Is Expanding Around the World

As noted, uranium is mined safely all over the world, including in several U.S. states. Although existing stocks are meeting current demand along with secondary sources, the uranium market could tighten significantly unless additional mines are explored. As new power plants are brought on-line, the U.S. could play a key role in meeting future demand with state and federal policies that allow entrepreneurs to invest in accessing uranium reserves. Of course, federal oversight agencies would still play an important role in protecting public safety.

In 2006, more than half of the world's uranium supply came from Canada, Australia and Kazakhstan, with Canada supplying one-fourth on its own. The U.S. accounted for only 4.24 percent of all uranium production. A decade ago, U.S. mines produced 2,400 tons of uranium and provided 1,100 jobs for American workers; these numbers dropped to as low as 1,100 tons and 321 jobs in 2003. Although production has increased steadily since then, the extent of proven reserves, especially in Wyoming and New Mexico, indicates that the U.S. could greatly contribute significantly to the forthcoming increase in demand for uranium.

Ultimately, estimates of the world's proven reserves are not 100-percent accurate, but figures indicate that Australia (35 percent) and Canada (13 percent) have considerably higher percentages of total world reserves than the United States (3–4 percent). According to the World Nuclear Association, most of the uranium in the United States is categorized as low-cost mining, which is an assessment based on the ease with which it can be mined and the quality of the ore.

Other former uranium mining countries are also considering the possibility of reentering the market; for instance, Finland, which has not mined the ore in 45 years. Finland currently receives 28 percent of its electricity from nuclear power and has a new plant under construction. The country is also implementing a comprehensive program to support its nuclear activities.

Mining Methods

Uranium is mined in one of three ways. Deposits up to 100 meters below the surface are generally mined through open-pit mining. Deeper reserves are normally accessed through underground mining. These underground mines are heavily ventilated to protect workers from radiation exposure. When the ore is of a high enough grade, it is sometimes partially processed underground to further protect workers from radiation exposure.

When conditions are right, a third method called in-situ leaching (ISL) can be very advantageous. This is the method most often used in the U.S. ISL entails dissolving the below-surface uranium into a low-acidic solution and then pumping it to the surface. This permits the extraction of uranium with minimal ground-level disturbance. Groundwater is then cleanly restored after the removal of uranium. Even as the U.S. imports approximately 80 percent of its uranium requirements, technological advancements in ISL have substantially lowered the costs of domestic mining.

The Milling Process

Once the ore is mined, it must be milled: the process by which the uranium is separated from other substances. These facilities are sometimes located near the mines.

Uranium is mined safely all over the world, including in several U.S. states.

The milling process depends on the state of the uranium when it is removed from the ground. Unless it was already leached, the ore must be crushed and treated with an acid solution to separate out the uranium. It is then further purified through a number of chemical processes. The resulting uranium-rich liquid is then dried into a powder called uranium oxide concentrate (U_3O_8), also known as yellow-cake. After further refinement, the yellow-cake is ready for the next steps in the fuel production process, which are separate from the mining/milling processes.

Mining Safety

Safety is and should be a paramount concern with uranium mining, especially in densely populated areas like Pittsylvania County. The reality is that the impact of uranium mining is not much different from the impact of other mining. For one thing, natural uranium is about as radioactive as granite. While there is often more dangerous radium or radon with uranium, these elements are safely managed to protect workers and the environment.

The two global leaders in uranium mining, Australia and Canada, have set the standard in workers' safety. Both countries have implemented strict regulations to control dust, minimize radiation exposure, and control for any significant radon exposure. Radiation doses are well below regulatory limits, according to the World Nuclear Association:

> Radiation dose records compiled by mining companies under the scrutiny of regulatory authorities have shown consistently that mining company employees are not exposed to radiation doses in excess of the limits. The maximum dose received is about half of the 20 mSv/yr limit and the average is about one tenth of it.

In the U.S., most environmental and operational oversight is conducted by the Environmental Protection Agency and the Nuclear Regulatory Commission. These agencies have found that both mining and ISL operations pose a low risk to the public.

Nuclear energy is becoming globally recognized as a safe, affordable, clean source of energy.

Mill tailings, the byproduct of the mining/milling process, are often the focus of safety concerns despite stringent regulation. Like uranium ore itself, the tailings differ with regard to radioactivity. During operations, the tailings are usually stored underwater to protect the environment from danger. Upon the cessation of mining activities, the tailings are safely managed through a number of proven methods, which usually involves returning them underground. Regardless of the method, the outcome is that surface radiation is returned to premining levels. Studies have demonstrated that the impact of tailings on humans is insignificant.

Reasonable Solutions

Another point of contention is the environmental footprint that uranium mining can leave. The waste from conventional open-cut mining and milling creates radioactive solid products that could pose a danger. However, these byproducts are managed in a safe and reasonable way that protects public health and the environment. Regardless of the mining method, the sites are restored and revegetated. In the case of ISL, because the only surface disturbance is bore-hole drilling, the site is easily restored to its original condition.

Nuclear energy is becoming globally recognized as a safe, affordable, clean source of energy. Uranium is an important and necessary component of nuclear energy, and firms choosing to pursue uranium mining should not be unnecessarily burdened by fear and government overreach. Uranium mining occurs all over the world, and the United States should realize its potential to increase America's share of the uranium mining sector. It has proven to be safe for workers, the public, and the environment and is critical to the ability of the U.S. to enjoy all of the advantages that accrue from expansion of nuclear power.

2

The Costs of Uranium Mining Outweigh Its Benefits

Al Gedicks

Al Gedicks teaches sociology at the University of Wisconsin-La Crosse and has written extensively on the impact of resource exploitation on indigenous peoples.

Proponents of nuclear power argue that it is a clean, "green" fuel source that does not contribute to the problem of global climate change. Nothing could be further from the truth. The process of obtaining and preparing uranium—the raw material essential for nuclear power—is heavily energy intensive. The mining, milling, enrichment and transportation of uranium all require massive quantities of fossil fuels, which release carbon dioxide into the atmosphere when they are burned. In addition to these hidden fossil fuel emissions, uranium mining and processing releases radioactive elements that harm both people and the planet. The heavy environmental costs of uranium mining are not worth the false promise of clean nuclear power.

Proponents of nuclear power argue that it does not produce carbon dioxide and thus does not contribute to global climate change. This argument, endlessly repeated by proponents of nuclear power, ignores the inconvenient fact that without the mining, milling and enrichment of uranium, there is no nuclear power. Each stage of the nuclear fuel cycle is extremely energy intensive and results in the emission of carbon dioxide into the atmosphere from the burning of fossil fuels.

Al Gedicks, "Nuclear Power's Costs Far Outweigh Its Benefits," *Milwaukee Journal Sentinel*, February 10, 2008. Reproduced by permission of the author.

The most energy-intensive stage of the nuclear fuel cycle is the mining and milling of uranium fuel. As the most accessible and higher grade uranium ores are mined, a greater amount of energy is required to extract uranium from less accessible and lower grade uranium concentrations.

After the ore is excavated by bulldozers and shovels, it must be transported by truck to the milling plant, consuming large amounts of diesel fuel. The uranium-bearing rock is then crushed and ground to a powder in electrically powered mills. The powder is then treated with harsh chemicals, usually sulphuric acid, to convert the uranium to a compound called yellow cake. Fuel is needed during this process to create steam and heated gases, and all the chemicals used in the mills must be manufactured at other chemical plants.

Energy Comes at a High Price

If the mill wastes, or tailings, which contain 85% of the original radioactivity in the ore, were to be disposed of properly by deep burial in the ground, additional quantities of fossil fuel would be required. Instead, these wastes are routinely dumped in large tailings piles on Native American lands, emitting radioactive elements into the air, water and soils, threatening human health and the environment in perpetuity. Communities near these tailings piles report a high rate of miscarriages; cleft palates and other birth defects; and bone, reproductive and gastric cancers as related health effects of uranium mining and exposure to contaminated air and water.

Proponents of nuclear power ... fail to recognize the substantial emissions of radioactive elements.

"This single remediation process, which should be scrupulously observed," says nuclear critic Helen Caldicott, "by itself makes the energetic price of nuclear electricity unreasonable."

Before uranium can be used in nuclear power plants it must undergo a process of enrichment. Uranium enrichment plants are the largest industrial plants in the world and consume enormous amounts of electricity. Far from being "clean," each 1,000-megawatt electric plant required the equivalent of a 45-megawatt electric coal plant—which annually burns 135,000 tons of coal—to supply its enrichment needs alone.

Uranium Mining Harms Native Americans

Proponents of nuclear power not only ignore the fossil fuel emissions of every stage of the nuclear fuel cycle, they also fail to recognize the substantial emissions of radioactive elements from this cycle and its disproportionate impact upon Native American lands and people.

There is no known way to safely dispose of this [radioactive] waste.

Over half of the nation's uranium deposits lie under Navajo and Pueblo Indian lands. At least one in five tribal members recruited to mine the ore were exposed to radioactive radon gas and have died and are continuing to die of lung cancer. The Navajo Nation banned uranium mining and processing on its land in 2005. Navajo President Joe Shirley Jr. said "it would be unforgivable to allow this cycle to continue for another generation."

Disposal Is a Problem

And what about nuclear waste disposal? Under current law, highly radioactive waste fuel must have a place to be stored permanently before a new reactor can be built in Wisconsin. There is no known way to safely dispose of this waste.

Are we going to dump the waste on the lands of the Western Shoshone Indians, as the federal government proposes to do at the Yucca Mountain site in Nevada? Are we going to dump the waste on the lands of the Menominee Indian Nation in Wisconsin, as the Department of Energy [DOE] tried to do in the 1980s? . . .

If Wisconsin's common sense moratorium on the construction of new nuclear power plants is lifted, the DOE will have all the more reason to reconsider the granite bedrock of Wisconsin's Wolf River batholith as a suitable site for a permanent nuclear waste repository.

3

Uranium Mining Exploits Indigenous People Worldwide

Brenda Norrell

Brenda Norrell is an Arizona-based writer who focuses on indigenous rights in the Americas.

The Indigenous World Uranium Summit in 2006 drew indigenous people from all over the globe—Australian aboriginals; villagers from India, Africa, and Asia; Pacific Islanders; and members of Indian tribes from the United States and Canada. They gathered to share information and call for a global halt to uranium mining, which disproportionately affects and endangers indigenous communities worldwide. Because they are small, marginalized cultures, indigenous peoples typically lack the political power and resources to fight exploitation. Banding together to create an international movement gives indigenous peoples a larger voice and makes their opposition to local mining projects more formidable. Attendees of the summit issued a formal statement calling for a global ban on uranium mining on native lands throughout the world.

Indigenous peoples from around the world, victims of uranium mining, nuclear testing, and nuclear dumping, issued a global ban on uranium mining on native lands.

The declaration, signed during the Indigenous World Uranium Summit, held Nov. 30–Dec. 2, 2006 on the Navajo Nation in Window Rock, Arizona, brought together Australian

Brenda Norrell, "Indigenous Peoples Call for Global Ban on Uranium Mining," *Counterpunch*, February 8, 2007. www.counterpunch.org. Reproduced by permission.

aboriginals and villagers from India and Africa. Pacific islanders joined with indigenous peoples from the Americas to take action and halt the cancer, birth defects, and death from uranium and nuclear industries on native lands.

Villagers from India testified to the alarming number of babies who die before they are born or [who] are born with serious birth defects, and of the high rates of cancer that are claiming the lives of those who live near the uranium mines.

Voices of Dissent

Australia Aboriginal Rebecca Bear-Wingfield, stolen as an infant and now an activist, told of the death threats for those who oppose the expansion of uranium mining in South Australia. Corporations have attempted to buy Aboriginals' approval for new uranium mining projects on native lands.

Aged Navajo uranium miners and their families continue to fight the Cold War in their doctor's offices.

From northern China came the voice of Sun Xiaodi, a whistleblower who has exposed massive unregulated uranium contamination. Xiaodi is now under house arrest in Gansu Province after he was "disappeared" and imprisoned in 2004–2005.

Xiaodi, along with five other anti-nuclear activists, was awarded the Nuclear-Free Future Award in 2006. The awards highlighted not only the personal and collective achievements of the recipients but also the international collaboration that has grown within the movement. Those honored came from several continents.

Organizing International Resistance to Uranium Mining

The Navajo Nation provides a fitting backdrop for discussions of the dangers of uranium mining. The history of uranium mining on these native lands goes back decades to when Navajo workers were sent to their deaths in Cold War uranium mines, unknowingly aiding the production of the world's first weapons of mass destruction.

Navajo Nation President Joe Shirley Jr. remarked, "As a result, radiation exposure has cost the Navajo Nation the accumulated wisdom, knowledge, stories, songs, and ceremonies—to say nothing of the lives—of hundreds of our people. Now, aged Navajo uranium miners and their families continue to fight the Cold War in their doctors' offices as they try to understand how the invisible killer of radiation exposure left them with many forms of cancer and other illnesses decades after leaving the uranium mines."

The rising price of uranium has caused renewed pressure on indigenous lands.

The tragedy spurred a growing resistance to the mines, and the Navajo Nation today is at the head of an international movement. In one of the movement's greatest achievements, in 2005 the tribe passed the Dineh Natural Resources Protection Act banning uranium mining on Navajo lands. Norman Brown, a Navajo and member of the organization Dineh Bidzill Coalition that co-organized the Summit, said, "The heart of this movement is here—we are at the center of this movement today."

Major Challenges

For years uranium mining was shrouded in secrecy as part of the Cold War and its victims were isolated.

Compensation has been hard to win in the courts and although recognized in the 1990 Radiation Exposure Compensation Act for Navajo Uranium Miners, only a small percentage of mining families have received their due.

A general lack of political power in indigenous communities makes them easy marks for dangerous uranium mining and dumping projects.

The rising price of uranium has caused renewed pressure on indigenous lands.

Like Navajos, Pueblos were also victims of the Cold War. As the truth emerged, Navajo and Pueblos in nearby New Mexico at first believed they were the lone victims of this death march. Uranium mining was enveloped in secrecy and carried out surreptitiously under the guise of national security, shielding it from public scrutiny and isolating its victims.

Global Networking

But as they became more vocal in their demands, the peoples of the U.S. Southwest soon met indigenous peoples from other parts of the world who shared similar histories as victims of uranium mining, nuclear testing, and nuclear waste dumps. Indignation grew as they realized that American Indian uranium miners in both the United States and Canada had been sent to their deaths to work in the uranium mines long after scientists warned of the health hazards of radon gas and radiation.

The first international meeting to exchange experiences and begin to develop demands took place at the World Uranium Hearing in Salzburg, Austria, in 1992, where activists began their struggle to halt uranium mining on indigenous land. In the words of the organizers, the Navajo meeting was held to follow up on that experience, develop coordinated actions and issue an international and energetic call for a halt to uranium mining on native lands throughout the world.

More than 300 participants from 14 countries participated in the event, with speeches covering all aspects of uranium mining, international activists efforts to halt the mining, and the devastating health effects.

Their message to the world: "Leave the uranium in the ground."

Global Threats to Local Life

At the Navajo summit, Manuel Pino, Acoma Pueblo from New Mexico and college professor, recalled that in Salzburg, Dene from Canada described the cancer that resulted from working in uranium mines without protective clothing. Mining in Canada and the United States was often carried out by the same corporations.

"As we went to Salzburg, we realized that many of our people were sick and dying," Pino said. He pointed out that Laguna Pueblo's Paguate village is only 2,000 feet from the largest open-pit uranium mine in North America, the Jackpile Mine. Pino said radioactive particles have been found in the animals, water, air, and in the bodies of people of the Pueblos.

Tribes must be vigilant to support one another in the protection of Mother Earth.

Residents of the Laguna Pueblo waged a pitched battle for reclamation of the Jackpile Mine. Originally owned by Anaconda, and now owned by Atlantic Richfield Company (ARCO) the lease owners simply walked away when mining stopped, leaving radioactive waste strewn and the earth torn apart. Ultimately, reclamation efforts began, but it was too late for the many Pueblos dying or already dead from cancer.

Pino noted that Acoma Pueblo members live downwind and downstream from the Grants, New Mexico, mineral belt—a 60-mile stretch where uranium was produced from 1948 through the 1990s. He claimed that most of the uranium mined on Indian lands by the United States Department of Defense was used in the production of weapons of mass destruction.

According to Pino, recent efforts endorsed by the United States and other nations to stall passage of the Declaration on the Rights of Indigenous Peoples in the United Nations stem from material interests. He stated that indigenous peoples have vast mineral resources beneath the surface of their lands, along with timber, water and other natural resources, and these nations view the exercise of indigenous rights as a threat to corporate access to and exploitation of this natural wealth.

"Our permanent sovereignty over our resources is a threat to the nation states of the world," Pino told the uranium summit.

He added that here on the Navajo Nation in the past the tribe has entered into leases that favor the corporations, often without being duly informed of the risks. In the Pueblos, he said, the people were never told of the harm that would result from the radioactive dust settling on their traditional drying fruit and drying meat.

Guardians of the Earth

Nation states, he said, do not realize that Indigenous Peoples take their responsibility as caretakers of Mother Earth seriously and will not back down. Recalling the words of [Sioux Chief] Sitting Bull, Pino urged the people to "come together to form a fist to protect Mother Earth."

Carletta Tilousi, Havasupai from the Grand Canyon in Arizona, attended both uranium summits, in Salzburg and Window Rock. Tilousi praised Havasupai tribal leaders for passing a ban on uranium mining in Havasupai territory in the Grand Canyon and placing the ban in the Havasupai Tribal Constitution.

Still, with the rising price of uranium and new threats to Indian lands, Tilousi said tribes must be vigilant to support one another in the protection of Mother Earth.

Coalition Gains Ground

Tilousi said the Havasupai like many other indigenous peoples felt very alone in their struggle until they went to Salzburg in 1992. There they met indigenous people from all over the world that are fighting mining corporations. On the Navajo Nation, Africans told of fighting gold mining corporations and indigenous peoples from the Pacific testified about nuclear testing that left behind radioactive fish.

"Those are the things that affect me very deeply," said Tilousi, who remembered her Havasupai elders and her Hopi relatives who have spent their lives struggling for indigenous rights and protection of Mother Earth.

Tilousi, who serves as a Havasupai tribal council delegate, said she admired the strength of the Navajos and others gathered at the conference. Recalling words that have long been repeated to her, she said, "Always keep Mother Earth in mind, always keep your spirit strong."

Speaking Out

Esther Yazzie-Lewis, Navajo, recalled her first trip to New York, when she was a young woman, decades ago, to speak out against uranium mining. She testified to how the uranium mined in Monument Valley, Arizona, on the Navajo Nation, was used to make the atomic bomb that killed Japanese in Nagasaki and Hiroshima. She remembered how the Japanese respected her for what she said that day and how good it felt to speak out.

Yazzie-Lewis recalled protesting in the cold on Navajo land, following the nation's largest uranium mill spill, in Church Rock, N.M. in 1979. At that time, not only were surrounding communities contaminated but in the years that followed Navajos living downstream at New Lands also became victims of radiation from the Church Rock spill. Ironically, they were living there after being relocated there from Black Mesa [Arizona] due to Peabody Coal's mining operations.

According to Yazzie-Lewis, the movement to oppose uranium mining employed many strategies and tactics. In addition to the direct action of protests at the mine, the opposition began to lobby local government. She cited in particular the late Harris Arthur, Navajo, and his work with the Navajo tribal government. Arthur's early efforts ultimately led to the Navajo Nation Council's passage of the Dineh Natural Resources Protection Act, the support of Navajo President Joe Shirley, Jr. and the Navajo Nation's ban on uranium mining

Global Solidarity

Yazzie-Lewis said her goal for the 2006 uranium summit was to create a global solidarity network. She encouraged indigenous peoples not to be fooled by the gifts of energy corporations, and to think of future generations.

"Let's protect what we have for our youths, so they will have the identity to be Navajos."

Navajos now have evidence to refute corporate claims that in-situ mining is safe and the water will not be harmed.

Mitchell Capitan, cofounder of Eastern Navajo Dineh against Uranium Mining, described the first efforts in eastern Navajo land in 1994. Capitan said his wife Rita was the main founder of the organization and promoted efforts to fight uranium mining at Crownpoint and Church Rock, N.M.

At the time, Capitan worked for Mobil Oil at an in-situ leach uranium mining demonstration project, six miles west of Crownpoint.

"It made me think that so much water was used, so much water was wasted and so much water was contaminated." After uranium prices plunged the project was shut down.

Mitchell, a lab technician for the project, said for three years Mobil attempted but could not restore the water to its original quality at the leach mining project site.

Secret Deals Uncovered

When there was renewed interest in mining in 1994, Navajos in Crownpoint took action. They discovered that secret negotiations were underway by corporations with landowners of non-tribal trust lands in this checkerboard land area. These were being carried out, without any public hearings. Navajos who were fighting to protect the water and air began to meet, with the first gathering attracting 40 community members.

"Ever since then, we began to roll," Capitan said, adding that Southwest Research and Information Center, based in Albuquerque, gave technical expertise.

Now, despite the Navajo Nation ban on uranium mining, corporations are planning new uranium mining in an area that would contaminate Navajos' drinking water in the Crownpoint and Church Rock areas, since the land is considered "checkerboard," with allotted lands and other non-trust lands intermixed with tribal trust lands.

Protecting the Water

But Capitan said Navajos now have evidence to refute corporate claims that in-situ uranium mining is safe and the water will not be harmed. They are fighting to protect the pristine aquifer water, which feeds two municipal deep wells providing water for 15,000 people.

"This is what we're trying to protect, our water. I hope we are not the guinea pigs of this in-situ leach mining. If they ever start mining in Crownpoint, the contamination of our water will take about seven years."

Capitan pointed out the strategy of corporations. In Crownpoint, the average income is $12,000 a year and the population is 97% Native American.

"The company is really using us. Sure, they say there will be plenty of jobs, but it doesn't take much manpower." He said in reality, the jobs would go to highly paid scientists, not local laborers. The people will be left with contaminated water.

"This kind of mining takes a lot of water, it would take our water," he said. Crownpoint people are working in a united effort to prevent uranium mining in nearby Church Rock because if the companies restart mining there the rest of the region will be threatened. "It will be a domino effect."

Power in Numbers

Capitan said that 12 years ago, when they began, he and his wife felt alone in the struggle and had little idea of where to look for help. Little by little, they became connected to an international movement that gave them greater leverage in the local battle.

"Word went out to the world; finally our Navajo Nation government listened."

The industry simply goes ahead and does what it wants.

Jamie Kneen of Minewatch Canada described the uranium mining and its effects on First Nations people in Canada. In Northern Ontario, mining and resulting contamination went on from the 1950s through 1990s. The Serpent River watershed water is now highly contaminated, which affects the Anishinaabe people. In Northern Saskatchewan the history is similar.

"In the [19]40s and 50s, the tailings were just dumped into lakes and rivers," Kneen recounted. Later, after tailing dams were in place, contaminated runoff became a hazard.

Efforts in Canada

Kneen reported that Canadian indigenous peoples have centered efforts on the processes for permits, consultation, and consent. In the regions of Canada where populations are primarily non-aboriginal and there is greater political influence with the government, communities have been able to halt the operations with bans on uranium mining. Public education and capacity-building in indigenous communities could increase their ability to do the same.

Another problem is getting industry to respond to the concerns of indigenous peoples. So far, Kneen stated, although Dene people have tried to slow the expansion of uranium mining in Canada, it has done little good. Public hearings have mostly failed to halt uranium mining.

"The industry simply goes ahead and does what it wants," Kneen said.

In Canada, he explained, the hard rock is full of cracks that contain water. Since water travels, the question is how water washed out of mining areas will seep into the system and affect the fish, wildlife and people.

The largest number of victims of uranium mining, nuclear testing and nuclear waste dumping were indigenous peoples.

Carrie Dann a Western Shoshone from Crescent Valley, Nev., told how Shoshone territory has been blighted by nuclear testing and is now targeted as a nuclear dump site at Yucca Mountain, which is under construction. Striving to protect their aboriginal lands granted by the Treaty of Ruby Valley of 1863, Western Shoshone are protesting nuclear testing. Now, gold mining corporations are hollowing out the mountains in Western Shoshone sacred land near Elko, Nev., in the area of Western Shoshone's sacred Mount Tenabo. The gold mining corporations began operations after the Dann's family horses were seized [by the U.S. Bureau of Land Management]. Currently, there is a resistance effort to halt the gold mining to protect the land and water.

Awards Honor Leaders

The Nuclear Free Future Awards were presented in cooperation with the Seventh Generation Fund and the International Physicians for the Prevention of Nuclear War, based in Germany. The Franz Moll Foundation for the Coming Generations presented the awards.

Claus Biegert of Germany, among the organizers of the event, said it was the tragedy of Chernobyl that triggered the uranium summits. After the catastrophe of Chernobyl, Biegert asked himself "What about the Navajo uranium miners who were dying and never made the news?" The world-famous disaster in Russia ended up revealing the silent deaths in Navajo land and other places. The common thread between the victims was a single mineral—uranium.

We have to let the world know that uranium should stay in the ground.

Biegert discovered that around the world, the largest number of victims of uranium mining, nuclear testing and nuclear waste dumping were indigenous peoples. This fact was first brought to his attention by a high school graduate readying for Harvard that he met in a cafeteria of the United Nations in Geneva in 1977. Her name was Winona LaDuke.

With a felt-tip pen, LaDuke had pointed out the uranium mining in the Southwest United States. She told Biegert if he was going to be involved, he should go to the Southwest, where she too would soon visit.

From those first efforts, the Nuclear Free Future Awards were born to recognize those fighting for justice around the world.

"We have to let the world know that uranium should stay in the ground," Biegert said to summit participants.

Activists Receive Recognition

The Nuclear Free Future Awards for 2006 were presented at the Navajo Summit. In addition to the award to Xiaodi other recipients included Gordon Edwards of Canada for educational activism, Wolfgang Scheffler and Heike Hoedt of Germany for global solutions with innovative green energy reflectors, and Ed Grothus of Los Alamos, N.M., for lifetime achievement for creative exposure of the nuclear industry.

There were two special recognition awards presented. Phil Harrison, Navajo, was honored for his struggle for justice and compensation by way of the 1990 Radiation Exposure Compensation Act for Navajo uranium miners. The Southwest Research and Information Center in Albuquerque was honored for the staff's relentless struggle for environmental justice.

Bringing Xiaodi's message to the summit was Chinese activist Feng Congde of Human Rights China in New York, who fled China after the massacre in Tiananmen Square in 1989. Xiaodi formerly worked in Project 792, referring to Uranium Mine No. 792—one of the highest yielding uranium mines in China. Opened in 1967, Project 792 was run by the military and annually milled 140–180 tons of uranium-bearing rock until it was officially shut down in 2002 as bankrupt owing to "ore exhaustion and obsolete equipment."

However, a private mine secretly rose from its radioactive ashes, operated by Longjiang Nuclear, Ltd. Its shareholders include a tight brotherhood of politicians and members of the nuclear ministry.

Report from China

"Just a couple of days ago, under the cover of night while the local Tibetans were all asleep, the mine as usual dumped untreated irradiated water straight into the Bailong River, a tributary of the Yangtze," said Xiaodi's written statement.

"At present, in our region there are an unusually high number of miscarriages and birth defects, with many children born blind or malformed."

He continued, "Today, large sweeps of Ansu Province—dotted with sacred sites—appear to have succumbed to an overdose of chemotherapy. The Chinese have taken no preventive measures to protect local human and animal life from uranium contamination," according to the award statement.

Tibetan workers report that an assortment of radioactivity-related cancers and immune system diseases account for nearly half of the deaths in the region. This remains among the "state secrets" and the patients' medical histories are manipulated to protect state secrecy.

Arrested for Speaking Out

Xiaodi asked that his $10,000 award be held for him, in hopes that he can someday be free to receive the award. His statement read, "Since my release from detention, I have been in an extremely insecure situation in which I am threatened, intimidated, and harassed. I felt tremendously honored and touched when I learned that I had been selected as this year's Nuclear Free Future Award recipient, because I have seen the great power of world peace and development.

"At the same time, I feel a deep sorrow, because I have also helplessly witnessed the environmental problems caused by the failure to effectively contain and reduce nuclear contamination.

"Breaking through fear to fight for a nuclear-free environment requires a person to take a path full of hardship, bloodshed, and tears, which could end up in either life or death. However, I firmly believe that if all people who are peace-loving and concerned with human destiny and upholding justice can come together and take action as soon as possible, a nuclear-free tomorrow can become a reality."

Activist Was "Disappeared"

On April 28, 2005 Xiaodi met with foreign journalists and told them about the frequent discharges of radioactive waste into Gansu waterways. He also told them about the Tibetan hitchhikers who climb up on trucks transporting uranium ore, happy for a ride. He also exposed that contaminated machinery was merely "hosed down" and sold to naïve buyers in Inner Mongolia, Xinjiang, Zhejiang, Hunan, and Hubei.

"These officials have blood on their hands," Xiaodi said.

The next day, plains clothes officers "disappeared" him. He was not heard from for months. Finally, mounting international pressure forced his release from Lanzhou Prison on Dec. 27, 2005.

Xiaodi continued to speak out against Project 792.

"They simply changed a military enterprise into a civilian enterprise and continued with large-scale mining." On April 4 [2006], Xiaodi visited fellow petitioner Yue Yongjim in prison. Xiaodi found Yongjim emaciated from forced labor on a food allowance of only three steamed flour buns a day. Xiaodi joined a protest demanding Yongjim's release. Xiaodi was again "disappeared," and is now under house arrest.

Call for a Global Ban

Grassroots organizers passed a declaration from the summit calling for a global ban on uranium mining on native lands. Further, indigenous vowed to take any action necessary, including direct action and court action, to halt uranium mining, nuclear testing and nuclear dumping on indigenous lands.

Indigenous peoples also set goals to contact stockholders of corporations violating the rights of indigenous peoples; increase media campaigns; educate fellow indigenous peoples on the issues; and to document abuses to the land and people.

4

Strong Government Oversight Makes Uranium Mining Safer Now

U.S. Environmental Protection Agency

The U.S. Environmental Protection Agency (EPA) is a federal government agency charged with protecting human health and the environment by writing and enforcing regulations based on laws passed by Congress.

Because uranium mining disturbs and releases radioactive substances during the extraction and milling processes, human exposure and environmental contamination are legitimate concerns that must be responsibly managed. In the decades since cancers and other ailments first appeared in uranium mine workers and community members who lived near mines, the government has tightened controls and has forced the uranium mining industry to improve its practices. There are now radiation protection standards in place to protect workers, pollutant discharge limits and drinking water standards to prevent groundwater contamination, laws to prevent mine tailings (waste) from being used as building materials, strict licensing and monitoring programs to regulate the practices of mining companies, and programs to identify and clean up contamination at abandoned uranium mines. Various government agencies at both the state and federal levels are involved in mining industry oversight and the enforcement of mandatory safety, health, and environmental standards to protect both the public and the natural world from the recognized dangers of uranium mining.

U.S. Environmental Protection Agency, "Uranium Mines," *RAD Town USA*, EPA Office of Radiation and Indoor Air, EPA 402-F-06-037, April 2006.

Uranium has been used in a variety of industrial and research processes. For example, uranium has been used as a coloring agent in decorative glass and ceramics, with uranium coloring found in glass from 79 AD. However, the greatest uses of uranium by far have been for defense and electric power generation.

The U.S. mining industry uses two distinct methods to extract uranium ore: physically removing the ore-bearing rock from the soil for processing or chemically dissolving uranium from the ore at the site.

Physically removing the rock ore generally involves either open-pit mining or underground mining.

- Open-pit mining is stripping away or excavating the topsoil and rock that lie above the uranium ore.

- Underground mining is extracting rock through a tunnel or opening [in] the side of a hill or mountain.

Chemically dissolving the uranium out of the rock ore is done through either heap leaching or in-situ leaching.

- Heap leaching is pouring chemicals over above-ground piles of crushed ore-bearing rock and collecting uranium through underground drains. This method is not used currently in the U.S.

- In-situ leaching, the most common method used in the United States, involves treating ore deep underground with chemicals to dissolve the uranium and then pumping the liquid to the surface through wells.

Radioactive Materials

The soils in these areas also contain uranium and radium, naturally occurring radioactive materials (NORM). Once exposed or concentrated by mining, this naturally-occurring material becomes Technologically-Enhanced NORM or TENORM. TENORM at mining sites consists of radioactive waste soils and rock, drill and corehole cuttings, and waste waters. Wastes at heap leaching or in-situ leaching operations are regulated by the U.S. Nuclear Regulatory Commission or its Agreement States and are classified as by-product materials rather than TENORM.

Milling is the process that removes uranium from the ore, which is mostly obtained in open-pit and underground mines. Once at the mill, the ore is crushed and ground up, and treated with chemical solutions to dissolve the uranium, which is then recovered from the solution. Tailings are the wastes from the millings processes and are stored in mill tailings impoundments, a specially designed waste disposal facility. These wastes are also classified as by-product materials.

Since 1879, when uranium mine workers began being diagnosed with lung diseases, such as cancer, regulators have gradually tightened controls and mandated improved uranium mining practices. Recently, officials also have become concerned with the broader impacts of uranium mining on public health and the environment.

Workers are directly exposed to the radiation hazards of uranium mines. There are radiation protection standards in place specifically to protect uranium mine workers.

Radiation and Mining

Uranium mining releases radon from the ground into the atmosphere. Open-pit and in-situ mining sites have been monitored by federal agencies and found to pose a low risk to the public. However, underground mines potentially pose a higher radon risk to both the public and workers. Mines and mining waste can release radionuclides, including radon, and other pollutants to streams, springs, and other bodies of water. Federal and state agencies have established pollutant discharge limits and drinking water standards, and continue to monitor these sites for public safety.

Uranium mine waste from operations that closed before the mid-1970s are of particular concern. In many cases, these mines remain unclaimed and the waste is still piled near the mine. Weathering can lead to radioactive dust that is blown by the wind and the seepage of contaminants into the surface and groundwater. There are also cases of unclaimed uranium mine waste being used for house construction, which creates significant radon and radiation hazard for inhabitants.

Regulators have gradually tightened controls and mandated improved uranium mining practices.

Radiation and Milling

Although the milling process recovers about 95 percent of the uranium present in ores, the residues, or tailings, contain several naturally-occurring radioactive elements, including uranium, thorium, radium, polonium, and radon. They also contain a number of chemically hazardous elements, such as arsenic. Past use of mill tailings for house, school, road, and other construction created public radiation health hazards. Those practices have been ended by the Uranium Mill Tailings Radiation Control Act which has been implemented by federal and state agencies.

Agencies That Regulate Uranium Mining

U.S. Environmental Protection Agency (EPA)

EPA established environmental protection standards for mill tailings under requirements of the Uranium Mill Tailings Radiation Control Act (UMTRCA).

EPA also has other standards and special programs that control radiation in operating mines and mills, in some old mines and mills, and in associated uranium-based products.

U.S. Nuclear Regulatory Commission (NRC)

NRC, or its Agreement States, license and oversee the operations of mills, heap, and in-situ leaching solution mines.

Mill sites regulated by NRC, NRC Agreement States, and the U.S. Department of Energy have waste holding areas under environmental protection standards established by EPA.

The States

Many states have signed formal agreements with NRC, delegating to the states regulatory authority over the licensing and operations of mills and in-situ leaching solution mines.

U.S. Department of Labor (DOL), Mine Safety and Health Administration (MSHA)

MSHA enforces compliance with mandatory safety and health standards to eliminate fatal accidents, reduce the frequency and severity of nonfatal accidents, minimize health hazards, and promote improved safety and health conditions in the nation's mines.

U.S. Department of Energy (DOE)

DOE takes control of closed and reclaimed mills, and reclaims some mill sites as authorized by Congress.

U.S. Department of the Interior (DOI), Bureau of Land Management (BLM)

BLM is responsible for managing 262 million acres of land—about one-eighth of the land in the United States—and about 300 million additional acres of subsurface mineral resources, including mines. The Office of Surface Mining provides funds to many state and tribal agencies for reclaiming uranium mines on their land for safety purposes.

U.S. Department of Agriculture (USDA), National Forest Service (NFS)

NFS reclaims abandoned mines in national forests.

U.S. Army Corps of Engineers (USACE)

The Corps of Engineers operates the Formerly Utilized Site Remedial Action Program (FUSRAP), which was originally established by DOE in 1974 to identify, investigate, and clean up contaminated sites formerly used by DOE's predecessor agencies. In some cases, these sites include mining and milling sites with radioactivity in levels above today's standards. FUSRAP covers many sites, including sites from the early years of the nation's atomic energy program. Through the FUSRAP, Federal agencies, state and local governments, and property owners work together to keep radioactive material on these sites under control. The Corps of Engineers has also assisted EPA and tribes in cleanup of abandoned mines on tribal properties.

How to Stay Safe Around Uranium

Government organizations continue to address potential threats from the uranium mining industry for the public health and safety but you can take actions as well for your own health and safety.

Uranium mine waste from operations that closed before the mid-1970s are of particular concern.

Workers in the industry have the potential for overexposure to radioactive material and must stay up-to-date on federal, state and industry health and safety guidelines. Following these procedures will reduce total on-site exposure. Workers also need to take precautions to avoid bringing radioactive material residue on their clothes and shoes home to their families and neighborhoods.

- Remove potentially contaminated clothes and shoes before returning to the family car and to your home or office.

- Do not bring home discarded equipment or material used at sites such as pipes, devices, bricks, rocks, and water or re-use these materials as containers or as building materials.

Members of the public should contact their local state geological survey or bureau of health to determine if there may be NORM and TENORM associated with uranium mining in their state or area where they live. Until then:

- Limit exposures and disturbance of the production site and any abandoned equipment.

- Do not handle, dispose, or re-use abandoned equipment from uranium mining sites.

You should never:

- Swim or drink the water from open pit mine lakes.

- Drink the water from streams and springs near abandoned uranium mines.

- Remove rock or soil from a uranium mine site for re-use or recycling for building construction.

- Take the rocks home as samples of souvenirs.

5

Uranium Mining and Nuclear Power Will Not Offset Climate Change

Mark Dowie

Mark Dowie is an investigative historian and award-winning journalist. He is the author of Losing Ground: American Environmentalism at the Close of the Twentieth Century.

Proponents of nuclear power claim that it is an ideal non-polluting energy source. While it is mostly true that a nuclear reactor does not create greenhouse gases or contribute much to global warming, that is only a small part of the picture. The true environmental impact of nuclear energy begins with finding, mining, milling, transporting and enriching uranium—all of which creates tons of harmful carbon dioxide emissions through the burning of fossil fuels. Even more energy is spent constructing nuclear power plants, generating power, and reprocessing and eventually storing depleted uranium and other nuclear wastes. These hidden environmental costs make it clear that uranium mining and the nuclear power it ultimately fuels will not offset climate change.

In 1990 the inland Inuit of Nunavut, a vast autonomous native region of northern Canada, voted almost unanimously to prohibit the prospecting and mining of uranium on their lands. They knew well the hazards of uranium from the experience of the Dine and other neighbouring tribes devastated

Mark Dowie, "Makings of a Nuclear Nightmare," *Daily Mirror*, March/April 2009. Reproduced by permission of *Resurgence* Magazine.

by previous mining ventures on their homelands. Uranium at the time was about US$7 a pound on the world market. Referendum aside, the calculus of mining, milling and shipping uranium ore almost anywhere in the world at that price was not much better than break-even. So the prospectors in Nunavut packed up and went home. But some things have happened to change their plans. The planet continued to heat up, carbon dioxide [CO_2] became recognised as a global toxin, and burning fossil fuels to make energy offered more evidence of human folly.

Before long the sagging, moribund but allegedly CO_2 [-free] industry of nuclear power was being reconsidered. A "nuclear renaissance" was predicted that would expand the global nuclear production from the current 438 power plants operating in thirty-one countries to over 1,000 by 2025. China and India have each announced plans to build scores of nuclear power plants, the tired old Washington nuclear lobby has been rejuvenated, and there is talk of a "hydrogen bonus"—using new nuclear capacity to produce hydrogen: fuel for a new clean and green economy.

The driving force of the "nuclear renaissance" is a claim that nuclear power, once up and running, is a carbon-free energy source.

Demand Outstrips Supply

Current world production of uranium is inadequate to the task. In 2004 global production was 46,500 tons of uranium oxide, whereas world consumption was 79,000 tons. The difference was made up with secondary sources: stockpiles, decommissioned weapons and recycled waste. But these are shrinking, so demand is growing for fresh sources of radioactive fuel. When US energy policy went nuclear, about the same time as some large mines flooded in Canada and Australia, hedge fund speculators dived into the market and uranium shot up to US$138 a pound, settling back eventually to about half that price, but still almost ten times the US$7 low. Within weeks of the price jump there were thousands of uranium claims staked around the world, hundreds of them in Nunavut.

One by one, newly formed prospecting companies helicoptered supplies into barren Arctic field-camps across the region, each staffed with geologists, engineers, pilots, cooks and as many Inuit helpers as possible. One camp opened in 2004; six more the following year. There were eight by 2006, and when I arrived in April 2008 there were twenty-eight uranium prospectors drilling the tundra of Nunavut. Huge milling companies from around the world, with names such as Uranor, Areva and Titan, had opened community liaison offices around the territory, all of them promising partnerships and royalties to impoverished Inuit villagers—and jobs. But the unemployment rate in some Nunavut communities is close to 70%.

"Nuclear Renaissance"

Aside from the combined intentions of countries like China, Russia, India, Finland and Italy to build hundreds of nuclear power plants over the next two decades, the driving force of the "nuclear renaissance" is a claim that nuclear power, once up and running, is a carbon-free energy source. The assertion is that a functioning nuclear reactor creates no greenhouse gases and thus contributes nothing to global warming or chaotic weather. That part is almost true, but the claim ignores the total environmental impact of nuclear energy, which includes a long and complicated chain of events known in the industry as the "nuclear cycle". The cycle begins with finding, mining, milling and enriching uranium, then spans through plant construction and power generation to the reprocessing and eventual storage of nuclear waste, all of which creates tons of CO_2. At every stage of the cycle greenhouse gases are released into the atmosphere from burning diesel, manufacturing steel and cement and, in the circumpolar regions of the planet, by disturbance of the tundra which releases huge amounts of methane, a particularly potent greenhouse gas.

It all begins with mining, which, together with milling of uranium (which almost always takes place near a mine) is a substantial CO_2 creator.

Even the claim that a functioning nuclear power facility is CO_2 free is challenged by the fact that an operating plant requires an external power source to run itself, and that electricity is almost certain to come from a fossil-fuelled plant. So the frequently repeated notion that nuclear power is a carbon-free energy source is simply untrue. The estimated contribution of atmospheric carbon from the entire nuclear cycle ranges from 5% to 30% of an equal power output from fossil-fuel generation, depending on who you ask and what they're comparing nuclear with.

Of course the nuclear industry, in its quest to appear pure and carbon-free, contests all such analysis, repeating an industry mantra that the nuclear cycle's carbon output is "about the same as solar". The truth almost surely lies somewhere in between those numbers and depends on how much fossil-fuelled power is used in milling, transportation, refining, construction, reprocessing and storage, and the carbon content of the fuel that is powering comparative systems. Either way, it all begins with mining, which, together with milling of uranium (which almost always takes place near a mine) is a substantial CO_2 creator.

The Carbon Footprints of a Mine

Every uranium mine has a different carbon footprint, depending on location, ore grade and distribution, depth of veins, and distance from mine to railhead. I asked as many mining

experts as I could find in Nunavut what the local carbon output of the large Kiggavik-Sissons deposit might be. No-one
was willing to hazard real numbers, but the extraction plan is
revealing.

Uranium ore will be mined from an open pit by huge
diesel-powered machines and trucks, transported by rail to
Churchill, Manitoba, then barged almost 1,000 kilometres to a
yet-to-be-constructed port on Baker Lake. From there it will
be transported up a seventy-five-mile all-weather road that is
also yet to be built. Fuel for the machinery and the mill will
be haulled into the site along the same road by diesel-fuelled
tanker trucks. All electricity at the mining camp will be provided by diesel-powered generators. The ore will be milled
and refined right at the mine site in a facility powered by diesel, and the resultant uranium oxide, known as yellowcake,
will be haulled to the Baker Lake port and tug-barged 1,000
kilometres back to the railhead at Churchill. In the winter
months, when Hudson Bay is frozen, yellowcake packed in
fifty-gallon drums will be flown from a yet-to-be-paved air-
strip to Toronto, then trucked to Port Hope, Ontario, where
most Canadian uranium is refined and shipped to reactors
around the world—never, according to national policy, to
weapons facilities.

> *Once touted as an energy source "too cheap to meter",*
> *nuclear power became ... "too costly to matter".*

Incidentally, if perchance one of those barges should over-
turn in a storm and a ton or so of yellowcake be released into
open water, the western shores of Hudson Bay would experience a major degradation to their ecosystems that would last
for thousands of years. And an inland radionuclide spill could
permanently poison the drinking water of caribou and Inuit
alike, as it has near so many former uranium mines around
the world, over 70% of them on indigenous lands.

A major challenge facing a resurgent nuclear industry is the astronomical and escalating capital cost of nuclear power and the clear negative return on investment. Wall Street investment bankers long ago backed away from underwriting nuclear energy and still won't touch it, nor will venture capitalists anywhere in the world. The US hasn't begun construction on a nuclear power plant for three decades. But a new generation of smaller, faster and allegedly much safer reactors are moving towards the drawing boards—eleven in nine US states. And there are currently thirty-one more licence applications before the United States Nuclear Regulatory Commission.

Politics and Power Plants

Former presidential candidate John McCain says the US should emulate France, where almost 80% of the energy is nuclear, and calls for forty-five new nuclear reactors to be built in the US by 2030, with a long-term goal of 100. And although defeated in the recent [2008] presidential election, he stubbornly refuses to support any energy bills lacking sufficient subsidies to meet those goals. [President] Barack Obama is not quite so sanguine about nuclear power, but his home town [Chicago] is ringed by eleven generating reactors, and he accepted generous campaign donations from Exelon, a leading nuclear construction firm, also headquartered in Chicago. Obama refuses to "eliminate nuclear power from the table".

Once touted as an energy source "too cheap to meter", nuclear power became, according to *The Economist*, "too costly to matter". In 1985, *Forbes*, America's most conservative business magazine, described the nuclear industry as "the largest managerial disaster in history". That's not the sort of publicity any industry needs in financial centres like London or New York where investors are trying to make, not lose money. Without finance capital, the entire global nuclear industry has become reliant on government support: in some countries, such as France and China, for the entire nuclear programme; in less socialist countries, such as the US, in the form of generous subsidies, loan guarantees and tax incentives to for-profit companies including Westinghouse, Bechtel, Exelon, Entergy and The Shaw Group, along with direct government investment in research and development, insurance and fuel processing.

The American nuclear industry, which now supplies about 20% of US electrical energy, has already received over US$145 billion in direct and indirect subsidies. That number will look small if the US government commits itself to a full nuclear renaissance, as the cost of nuclear construction, in constant dollars, is now three times what it was in 2001 when *The Economist* declared it too costly to matter. And that's a conservative estimate. An Areva-designed Evolutionary Power Reactor (the current rage) sells for US$3–4 billion, twice the price of a coal plant producing the same kilowatts. But throw in construction costs, delays, over-runs and interest, and we're looking at something closer to US$8–9 billion per plant.

Mining . . . is the easy way out. And we're moving too quickly to embrace it.

Whatever the cost of an individual plant, a nuclear revival simply cannot happen, anywhere in the world, with out massive government support. The nuclear industry does not deny the subsidies, or claim that it could survive without them. Its argument is that almost everything worthwhile in a complex economy, including wind and solar power, and now banking and finance, need to be subsidised somehow.

Cultural Considerations

Before I left the barren, windswept reaches of the far north, I visited Sheila Watt-Cloutier, former President of the Inuit Circumpolar Conference, a multinational council representing the 150,000 Inuit living in Alaska, Canada, Russia and Greenland. She was a nominee for the Nobel Prize in 2007. Her modest Iqaluit home is perched on the shoreline of Frobisher Bay, which was still frozen solid in May. As we chatted about Inuit culture and circumpolar politics. I watched Inaluit hunters and fishermen heading down the sparkling sunlit Frobisher ice field in dog sleds and snowmobiles. One was driven by her son-in-law, Qajaac Ellsworth, who was taking her only grandson on his first hunt, a vital rite of passage in any native community. Watt-Cloutier beamed with pride, but she was apprehensive about the future of Inuit culture, as technology and industry offer their alluring enticements. She is opposed to neither, but is concerned about the speed of their approach, as her people experience the jarring transition, shared by so many indigenous people around the world, from a traditional land-based hunting culture to a modern wage-based economy.

She is reluctant at first to speak out against uranium, even though the Inuit Circumpolar Conference still advocates a "nuclear-free Arctic". Later in the afternoon she relents and agrees to discuss, ever so cautiously, what is clearly a sensitive topic in Nunavut. "Mining", she believes, "is the easy way out. And we're moving too quickly to embrace it. It could run counter to everything we are trying to do to recover our culture. We need to step back and ask ourselves what kind of society we are trying to create here. Will we lose awareness of how sacred the land is, and our connection to it? Do we abandon or rebuild institutions we have relied on for generations? Or are we just going to allow ourselves to become dependent on new industries, substances and systems?" She pauses for a moment to watch the hunters head down Frobisher Bay, and then turns back for one last question: "Do we want to lose the wise culture we have relied on for generations?"

The answers to these questions are of vital consequence, not just to the Inuit but to the whole world. Even if the expansion of the US and European nuclear industries is delayed by economic troubles at home, that won't likely stop China, India and other developing nations from expanding their nuclear programmes. No matter what form it takes, one thing seems clear: if the nuclear renaissance is going to happen, uranium mining is going to expand, and indigenous people like the Inuit of Nunavut will bear a considerable proportion of its ill effects.

6

Uranium Mining Can Boost Local Economies

William M. Welch

William M. Welch is a staff writer for USA Today, *a daily newspaper with national circulation.*

Small towns in New Mexico that thrived during the first uranium boom—and fell on hard times with the industry's decline—are poised to be economically reinvigorated by the renewed interest in nuclear power. As the price of uranium has skyrocketed along with demand, so has interest in reopening old uranium mining claims and locating promising new supplies of the element that fuels nuclear power plants. Dozens of mining companies have already entered the market, and many former uranium workers who remember fat paydays during the last boom are eager to cash in by going back to work in new or reopened mines. Many economically depressed communities welcome a revived uranium mining industry because it means a revived local economy.

Like a lonely Maytag repairman, Joe Lister has spent the past 16 years keeping quiet watch over a half-mile hole in the ground on an extinct volcano outside town [Grants, New Mexico].

Lately, though, his phone has been ringing. A lot.

The Mount Taylor mine where Lister is manager and caretaker sits on one of the nation's largest reserves of uranium.

William M. Welch, "Boom Times for Uranium Mines?" *USA Today*, July 10, 2007. Reprinted with permission.

And with a uranium renaissance at hand, old-timers who once worked the mines are checking in from all over, eager to pick up helmets and picks that lay untouched for decades.

"They call me from jail, home, the bar and say, 'Joe, when's the mine opening? Have you got a job for me?'" says Lister.

Soon, he hopes—a hope shared by a generation of old mining hands. Grants and other towns west of Albuquerque recall the yellow ore not as fuel for nuclear plants and atomic bombs but for its conversion to cash.

Remembering Good Times

"It was big money," says Frank Emerson, who arrived in New Mexico from Montana half a century ago looking for a job in the mines. He expected "I'd be here long enough to get a stake," and never left.

Miners drew a wage and also were paid bonuses tied to production. Even in the '50s, some could make $80,000 a year—and spend it.

Old-timers who once worked the mines are checking in from all over, eager to pick up helmets and picks that lay untouched for decades.

"People went through their money like water," says former miner Cecil Brown.

"We had 21 bars here at one time, and 21 service stations and one street," says 85-year-old Ralph McQueary, who owned two of those gas stations.

Emerson says he "made money like a yo-yo, up and down," before he ran for municipal judge and won. Now retired, he and a lot of men who went through boom and bust in this dusty town, encircled by mesas and cut through by Route 66, smell good times again.

This time, it is the exploding price of uranium ore.

Trading at $7 a pound in 2001, "yellowcake," as it is called, hit $120 a pound in May [2007]. By the end of June it raked in as much as $138 a pound on the spot market.

The surging price has lured more than two dozen companies with mining expertise to the high-desert uranium fields here in just the past year or so, says John Indall, a Santa Fe lawyer for the Uranium Producers of America. The companies are reviving old claims, searching filing cabinets for forgotten geological maps and hiring old-timers who know the land.

"We have seen a kind of gold rush," says William von Till, chief of the Uranium Recovery Branch at the Nuclear Regulatory Commission (NRC) in Washington [D.C.].

> *The surging price has lured more than two dozen companies with mining expertise to the high-desert uranium fields.*

Von Till says prices are propelled by a belief among energy markets that nuclear power is poised for a revival. The NRC expects orders for as many as 28 new reactors over the next two years, and scores more are planned worldwide over the next decade, says Larry Camper, director of the division of waste management and environmental protection at the agency.

Renewed Interest in Nuclear Power

Why the comeback? Increasing demand for energy in developed and underdeveloped nations, coupled with worries that coal- and oil-fired power plants may contribute to global warming. Nuclear power produces zero greenhouse gases, and the USA has a massive supply of uranium.

Uranium rose as an industry in the West in the post-World War II atomic age. But production withered to almost nothing by the mid-1980s after nuclear accident scares at Three Mile

Island in Pennsylvania and Chernobyl in the former Soviet Union shook public faith in nuclear power.

Many Navajo landowners need the money uranium can bring.

Uranium is found widely, but New Mexico is the mother lode. Indall estimates that 600 million pounds of uranium lie under New Mexico's sandy soil. And the energy produced by a pellet of uranium the size of a fingertip is equal to that produced by nearly a ton of coal, Lister says.

Yet not everyone is hankering for a uranium boom.

Navajo Nation President Joe Shirley signed a tribal law two years ago banning mining on Navajo lands, which cover much of rural New Mexico. He says the last boom left behind radiation, pollution and disease.

"I believe the powers that be committed genocide on Navajo land by allowing uranium mining," he said.

Not all Navajos agree.

In Crownpoint, a small town along a mesa that is part of the Navajo Nation, resident Ben House says many Navajo landowners need the money uranium can bring. He is working for one of the companies, HRI Energy of Lewisville, Texas, pursuing claims.

"Right now the economy is very bad in Crownpoint. We don't even have a café," he says.

Grants once counted 18,000 residents, but when mining left so did the people. The population is now 8,000. The town brought in jobs, in part, by bringing in prisons. There are now three prisons here, one federal and two state—one of them for women.

Uranium is what brought people to Grants and to many small towns around this southernmost tip of the Rockies. And uranium is what ran it down.

Reason to Be Cautious

Reminders of the boom-gone-bust are all around Grants. A shuttered restaurant bears the sign "Uranium Café." Old drilling equipment sits on display outside a mining museum. Trucks at a dry desert patch, unfittingly named Ambrosia Lake, work to entomb a massive pile of sandstone, also known as tailings, left behind by a once-thriving uranium operation.

Kelly Cregger, 78, moved here from Wytheville, Va.—and from West Virginia's coal mines. Eventually, he got mad at a local judge and ran against him. They tied, and the winner was decided by pulling names from a hat. Cregger won, becoming a judge like his friend Emerson. He didn't have a law degree, but he now had a regular paycheck. He could hardly believe it.

"My folks back there in Virginia couldn't hardly believe it, either," Cregger says.

Salvador Chavez took a mining job in 1969. When uranium played out, he went to work for the state highway department, but kept collecting geological maps drawn up by the old mining companies showing where the uranium lay.

A few months ago, HRI and a Japanese partner hired Chavez for his experience, and his maps. Today, he drives a new luxury Lincoln pickup with the license plate "U308"—the chemical symbol for yellowcake.

Like the old days, uranium is roping them in again from all over.

"My love is underground," says Rick Van Horn, a Texas miner who arrived in town in January. "There is nothing like it. You always know what the weather will be like."

7

Uranium Mining Is an Economic Dead End

Susan Montoya Bryan

Susan Montoya Bryan is a writer for the Associated Press, a newspaper wire service.

The renewed interest in nuclear power has led to a renewed interest in uranium mining in western New Mexico and to excitement about the jobs and money it could bring the economically depressed region. A recent study, however, describes the mining industry's optimistic projections of economic stimulus from uranium mines as "a gross exaggeration." Because the uranium industry operates on a "boom or bust" cycle, it is unlikely that mining that is profitable to the community can be sustained for more than a few years. Once the industry is reestablished and people come to again depend on uranium mining as a source of income, the industry's failure or withdrawal from New Mexico could further devastate a vulnerable region that is still suffering the economic fallout from the collapse of the first uranium boom. The promise of a short-term profit is not enough to offset the possible long-term consequences.

An environmental group is challenging claims that a rebirth of the uranium mining industry in western New Mexico would return thousands of jobs and billions of dollars to a region still hurting from the collapse of the last uranium boom.

A study commissioned by the New Mexico Environmental Law Center contends estimates that the industry would bring

Susan Montoya Bryan, "Benefits of Uranium Mining Debated," *Santa Fe New Mexican*, November 2, 2008. Reprinted with permission of the Associated Press.

$30 billion and more than a quarter of a million jobs to the state are "a gross exaggeration."

Eric Jantz, the center's staff attorney, said the impetus for doing the report was to get a realistic perspective on whether the economic benefits of renewed uranium mining in New Mexico would outweigh environmental and health concerns.

Boom and Bust Cycles

"The ultimate conclusion of the report is that the landscape has an inherent value and clean air and water have inherent values. They're the economic driver for the region and New Mexico," Jantz said. "Those things are sustainable, whereas the uranium industry and every other extractive industry are subject to boom and bust cycles."

But James Peach, a professor at New Mexico State University who studied the potential impacts for the industry, said the economic expectations are reasonable when considering that uranium companies plan to do business in the state for at least the next three decades.

Several companies showed an interest in western New Mexico's ore when prices skyrocketed last year. Despite a recent drop to less than $50 per pound, two companies have exploratory drilling applications pending with state regulators.

The uranium industry and every other extractive industry are subject to boom and bust cycles.

The Environmental Law Center's report, released last week, states that the industry bases its economic claims on assumptions the price of uranium would return to the $90 to $100 per pound range and stay there indefinitely.

Industry Refutes Criticism

Peach said he used the long-term contract price of uranium rather than the spot price to gauge the economic impact. He said about four-fifths of all uranium sales are based on a contract price, which stands at about $80 per pound.

Peach also noted today's market is global, with 30 countries using nuclear power and a few dozen more building or planning to build nuclear power plants.

People who could benefit in the short term from a paycheck could end up paying a high price.

"The data clearly indicates that U.S. and world uranium requirements for nuclear power generation far exceed current and projected production levels," Peach said, meaning a high price for ore could be sustainable.

The Environmental Law Center argues that the uranium industry, like other commodities, operates on a boom and bust cycle that could leave western New Mexico vulnerable, as it was when the mines began to close in the 1980s and more than 6,000 jobs were lost.

But Star Gonzales, director of the Cibola Communities Economic Development Foundation, said Grants—a town once known as "the Uranium Capital of the World"—learned from the last bust and is prepared for both the ups and downs of the cycle.

She said renewed mining in the area would spur economic development in her community, where gas stations and other stores along main street have long been boarded up.

"They're wrong in saying that it's too good to be true," she said. "I think that the industry will benefit our community. . . . For every one mining job, there's probably going to be four created."

Costs Are Not Just Economic

Despite the potential economic benefits, critics say the environmental and social costs must be considered.

According to the center's report, the federal government expects to spend nearly $100 million on monitoring and maintenance at past uranium mining sites across the country over the next six decades.

The report also states the federal government has paid about $625 million to former uranium workers or their families for diseases and deaths associated with exposure to radiation while working in the industry between 1942 and 1971.

Jantz said people who could benefit in the short term from a paycheck could end up paying a high price.

"I don't know why people think that a renewed uranium boom would be any different," he said. "Maybe things were OK in Grants for a while but where's the uranium mining industry now? They want the resources but they haven't been taking care of the folks in Grants for the last 20 years."

Gonzales, who also is director of the Grants Chamber of Commerce and curator of the community's Mining Museum, said the industry now faces more rigorous standards and has improved methods for mining ore.

"I'm not just taking it for face value," she said of the industry's promises. "We've researched this. Certainly I wouldn't advocate anything that was going to be harmful to my community. I live here too."

8

Uranium Mining Threatens National Parks

Dusty Horwitt

Dusty Horwitt is a Public Lands Analyst for the Environmental Working Group, a nonprofit organization that aims to protect public health and the environment.

The renewed interest in nuclear power has led to a land rush in the American Southwest, as scores of mining companies stake claims in hopes of cashing in on a uranium boom. Many of the country's national parks and wild lands are jeopardized by this activity. Since 2003, more that 4,700 mining claims have been opened within five miles of national parks and monuments; a substantial number are uranium mines. The 1872 Mining Act, which allows mining on public lands with little formality, is no longer sufficient to protect our most treasured natural resources. Oil and petroleum companies are required to go through a much more strict process to operate on public lands; uranium mining should be no different. The Mining Act should be updated to protect important natural sites, set tougher standards for mine permits and cleanup, treat mining the same as oil and gas exploration, ensure a fair return to taxpayers through royalties, end mining tax breaks, establish an abandoned mine cleanup fund and ban the practice of buying claimed land from the federal government.

Dusty Horwitt, "Statement of Dusty Horwitt, JD: Public Lands Analyst, Environmental Working Group," *Senate Committee on Energy and Natural Resources*, September 27, 2007. Reproduced by permission of Environmental Working Group.

For the last several years, the Environmental Working Group has analyzed mining claims on federal land, using computerized data provided by the Bureau of Land Management [BLM]. . . .

What we have found is a frenzy of claim staking that is escalating each day and threatens a crisis for many of America's most treasured wild places and national parks, including the Grand Canyon, where there has been an explosion of uranium mining claims. This modern-day land rush is driven by the sky-high price of uranium, gold and other metals caused by demand from China, the United States and players around the globe.

Since 2003, claims on all public land in 12 Western states have increased by 80 percent. This dramatic surge in claims could be extremely problematic because once a claim is staked, the federal government interprets mining law as providing virtually no way to stop hard rock mining at that site, short of buying out mining claims or other congressional intervention, even when mining is in plain view of national parks such as the Grand Canyon. . . .

Under the current, wide open mining law, vast portions of the American West are at the mercy of global demand for minerals.

A valid mining claim gives the claim holder the opportunity to mine on federal land and can be staked without government approval or oversight wherever land is open to mining. This Wild West approach stands in stark contrast to the approval required through the oil and gas leasing program where the public has an opportunity to participate in decisions that affect public lands. As anyone knows who has been in the West in the past five years, this approval process has not in any way stymied oil and gas exploration.

Mining Law Needs Reform

More than four years of analysis of mining claims has led us to one inescapable conclusion: Under the current, wide open mining law, vast portions of the American West are at the mercy of global demand for minerals. This is simply unacceptable. Without changes to the law, global demand for minerals could easily result in situations where companies begin prospecting and developing mining claims right next to incomparable wonders like the Grand Canyon, other national parks and wilderness areas, or even local water supplies.

Globalization has finally caught up with the 1872 Mining Act and rendered it totally and definitively obsolete. The West is not as big as it used to be. With growing demand for metals we do not need a Mining Law designed to encourage mining; we need a mining law that both permits mining, but also protects, without wavering, our most important natural places and resources.

We need a mining law that both permits mining, but also protects, without wavering, our most important natural places and resources.

More Mining Claims Than Ever

Our research shows that in 12 Western states, the number of active mining claims has increased from 207,540 in January 2003 to 376,493 in July 2007, a rise of more than 80 percent. Over an eight-month period, from last September [2006] to this May [2007] the BLM recorded more than 50,000 new mining claims. Claims as of July 2007 covered an estimated 9.3 million acres.

We have seen this increase in every Western state, with claims for all metals increasing by 50 percent or more in Arizona, Colorado, New Mexico, Nevada, South Dakota, Utah and Wyoming. [. . .]

Many of the new claims are for uranium. The BLM reports that the estimated number of uranium claims staked in Colorado, New Mexico, Utah and Wyoming combined increased approximately 750 percent from less than 4,300 in fiscal year 2004 to more than 32,000 in fiscal year 2006.

Many of the claims for all metals are being staked by foreign mining companies and speculators who could mine the land or sell to multinational corporations. Mining companies often extract minerals using techniques involving toxic chemicals, giant earthmoving equipment, sprawling road networks and vast quantities of water where water is a precious, scarce resource.

This land rush is sweeping the West despite the remnants of an earlier generation of uranium mines that have left a legacy of death and disease, despite the fact that mining as a whole is our leading source of toxic pollution and despite the fact that mining claims give companies a right to mine that effectively supercedes efforts to protect the environment and preserve our American heritage.

In the face of a landslide of global economic forces that threaten many of our most valued natural places and the health of people all across the American West, the 1872 Mining Law offers the legal equivalent of a pick and a shovel. . . .

Mining Claims Near National Parks

As of July [2007], mining interests held 815 claims within five miles of the [Grand Canyon National] Park, 805 of them staked since January 2003. Many of these claims are for uranium.

A Canadian company, Quaterra Resources, has already proposed to drill exploratory bores for uranium on claims just north of the Canyon. The operation would include a helicopter pad to carry supplies in and out. The idea of uranium mining near America's greatest national treasure is troubling and the thought of helicopter flights of radioactive material in an area already crisscrossed by dozens of tourist flyovers a day is even more disconcerting.

This land rush is sweeping the West despite the remnants of an earlier generation of uranium mines that left a legacy of death and disease.

The same explosion of claims has occurred in the canyon country of southern Utah and Colorado.

Many of these claims are also for uranium. Arches National Park in Utah has 869 claims within five miles of its boundary, 864 of them staked since January 2003. Nearby, Canyonlands National Park has 233 claims within five miles, all staked since January 2003. Many of the claims on the Colorado side are near lands treasured for their scenic and recreational values. . . .

Without proper safeguards for our public lands, protecting national parks from these claims can be very costly. . . .

The Legacy of Uranium Mining

The Department of Energy has begun a project to clean up 16 million tons of radioactive uranium mine waste near Moab [Utah] that have contaminated land near the Colorado River. The waste is a threat that could pollute drinking water for millions. Cleanup estimates range between $412 million and $697 million and, according to the Department of Energy, the project could last until 2028.

You'll also note the town of Monticello, Utah. . . . Colorado's Grand Junction *Daily Sentinel* recently reported that residents of Monticello claim unusually high rates of cancer they believe were caused by a now-closed uranium mill.

The *Los Angeles Times* reported in a landmark series last year [in 2006] how uranium mining has left a legacy of cancer and a degenerative disease known as Navajo Neuropathy on the Navajo reservation that includes Arizona, Colorado, Utah and New Mexico.

In Situ Leaching

Uranium mining companies have said that a process called "in situ leaching" will reduce environmental harm, but the practice raises significant concerns about contamination of groundwater according to the U.S. Geological Survey (USGS) and Nuclear Regulatory Commission (NRC). In this type of mining, chemicals are injected underground to leach uranium out of subterranean deposits. While the USGS and NRC state that in situ leaching "in general" is less harmful than traditional uranium mining and milling, "the use of leaching fluids to mine uranium contaminates the groundwater aquifer in and around the region from which the uranium is extracted." The agencies add that "groundwater restoration represents a substantial portion of the cost of decommissioning at a uranium leach mining facility." . . .

When mining threatens to scar if not destroy places like the Grand Canyon, it is time to draw the line.

Antiquated Law

The threat we face today, however, is more serious than in years past. The specter of mining operations is looming over the Grand Canyon and many other treasured national parks, and the 1872 Mining Law provides inadequate tools to control it. Indeed, the 1872 Mining Law does the opposite: it directly facilitates the problem by granting mining rights with no government approval, providing weak standards for protecting water, and creating a potential bonanza with no royalty payments if the claim pans out. Under current law, demand for raw materials around the globe can place our public lands at risk and leave Westerners and federal land managers at the mercy of multinational mining companies.

Mining companies have argued against changing the law because mining is so important to our national security. Yet the oil and gas industry is also vital to our national security and has operated on federal land under a significantly different set of rules. Oil and gas operators must win government approval before gaining control of federal land, pay royalties on the energy they extract and are subject to rules that allow energy development to be balanced with other interests. Under this system, oil and gas companies have enjoyed record profits and record numbers of approvals for drilling permits in the past several years. Indeed, government oversight has often been far too lax. But the main point is that the oil and gas industry has thrived under a much more progressive legal framework.

Mining has operated under an antiquated law for long enough. When mining threatens to scar if not destroy places like the Grand Canyon, it is time to draw the line. We no longer need to give special treatment to the mining industry, particularly when other extractive industries operate profitably on our public lands without such favored treatment and particularly when our national parks and monuments are at risk.

Recommendations to Improve the Mining Law

We recommend several changes to the mining law:

- *Protect Western lands*: Mining companies should be allowed to operate on federal lands, but some places should be off-limits. These places include lands bordering National Parks, Forest Service Roadless Areas, and sacred sites.

- *Tougher standards for mine permits and cleanup*: Mining companies should be required to prevent perpetual water contamination and put up enough money before operations begin to cover the full costs of cleanup should the company go bankrupt or abandon the site.

- *Treat Mining Like Oil and Gas*: Land managers should have the ability to balance mining with other interests such as water quality, the same ability they have with oil and gas and other extractive industries.

- *Royalty payments*: Currently, mining companies pay no royalty unlike every other extractive industry operating on federal land. A fair return to taxpayers is essential for cleaning up abandoned mines and providing assistance for communities affected by the boom and bust mining economy.

- *Abandoned mine cleanup fund*: Cleaning up abandoned mines is estimated to cost $32 billion or more. Congress should create a fund to accomplish this important task.

- *An end to mining's tax break*: In addition to being able to mine royalty-free, mining companies can claim a tax break on up to 22 percent of the income that they make off hardrock minerals mined on federal, public lands. Congress should close this loophole.

- *No more land giveaways*: For years, mining interests have been able to buy claimed land from the federal government for $2.50 or $5.00 an acre. Since 1994, Congress has placed a moratorium on these giveaways that must be renewed annually. Congress should enact a permanent ban.

Mining provides materials essential to our economy, but it must be conducted in a way that strikes a balance with other values.

9

Grand Canyon Uranium Mining Could Jeopardize the Colorado River

Mark Clayton

Mark Clayton is a staff writer for the Christian Science Monitor.

If they are allowed to operate, thousands of uranium mines near Grand Canyon National Park could contaminate the Colorado River and threaten the drinking water supply of millions of people. Despite mining industry assurances that improved mine practices minimize the potential for such ecological disaster, the location is too critical and the water supply too important to take a chance. Even when best practices are followed at the mines, nature itself can have a hand in spreading radioactive contamination from uranium mines; heavy rains and flooding can easily wash uranium into the river and the groundwater supply. Because the consequences of such contamination would be so dire and long-lasting, Congress is working on legislation to permanently ban uranium mining on federal land around Grand Canyon National Park.

On a ragged outcrop just a short walk from a Grand Canyon overlook where millions of visitors annually come to gawk at one of the world's most stunning vistas sits the old Orphan uranium mine. Soil radiation levels around it are 450 times higher than normal. It's encircled by a protective fence.

Mark Clayton, "Do Uranium Mines Belong Near Grand Canyon?" *The Christian Science Monitor,* August 19, 2008. Copyright © 2008 The Christian Science Publishing Society. All rights reserved. Reproduced by permission from *Christian Science Monitor,* (www.csmonitor.com).

A sign warns: "Remain behind fence—environmental evaluation in progress." In the canyon hundreds of feet below, another sign by gurgling Horn Creek instructs thirsty hikers not to drink its radioactive water.

Even so, Horn Creek eventually splashes its way to the canyon bottom and into the Colorado River, a vital water source for 25 million people from Las Vegas to Los Angeles to San Diego. In that mighty river, the Orphan's radioactive dribble is diluted to insignificance.

Mining companies have staked more than 10,600 exploratory mineral claims . . . spread across 1 million acres of federal land adjacent to the Colorado River and Grand Canyon National Park.

But what if a dozen or even scores of new uranium mines were leaching uranium radioisotopes into this critical water source? That is what Arizona's governor, water authorities in two states, scientists, environmentalists, and Congress are all worried about. Should they be?

Could It Happen Again?

Everybody from mining-industry officials to environmentalists agrees that the Orphan mine is a poster child for the bad old days of uranium mining going back to the 1950s. Today's regulations and newer mining techniques make such pollution far less likely, industry officials say, though environmentalists vehemently disagree. The question remains: Is Orphan only a vision of the past—or is it a vision of the future, too?

The US Southwest may be about to find out. Driven by soaring uranium prices and fresh interest in nuclear power, mining companies have staked more than 10,600 exploratory mineral claims—most of them smaller than five acres—spread across 1 million acres of federal land adjacent to the Colorado

River and Grand Canyon National Park, a federal official told Congress in June [2008]. Most are uranium claims, though some may be for other metals, observers say.

Such numbers and testimony about pollution have begun to move Congress. Following congressional hearings, the House Natural Resources Committee in late June [2008] declared an emergency withdrawal of 1 million acres from any mining claims. The federal land in question is on the north and south rims of the Grand Canyon, just outside the national park, through which the Colorado River flows.

While a federal lawsuit and injunction have temporarily stalled uranium development in the national forest on the south rim, Congress's action is being resisted by the [George W.] Bush administration on the north rim.

The question of what impact dozens of new uranium mines across the entire Colorado River watershed might have ... remains hotly debated.

There, lands controlled by the Bureau of Land Management [BLM] are unaffected by the lawsuit to the south and exploration claims are still being processed routinely.

One such claim, by Quaterra Alaska Inc., the US subsidiary of Vancouver-based Quaterra Resources, Inc., was approved for exploratory drilling on June 27 [2008]—just two days after the House's Natural Resources Committee vote that should have stopped such action.

A Department of Interior spokesman says the BLM is still processing claims because the agency doesn't consider the Congressional vote valid. In a July [2008] letter it argued that the committee didn't have a quorum, a point disputed by the committee's chairman and the House parliamentarian.

Mining Regulations Are Tougher Now

"They are charging forward," says Taylor McKinnon, public lands director for the Center for Biological Diversity, an environmental group based in Tucson, Ariz.

Last month [July 2008], the US Department of Energy approved 42 square miles for an expanded uranium mining program in the watershed of the Dolores River, a tributary of the Colorado. But the question of what impact dozens of new uranium mines across the entire Colorado River watershed might have—an environmental disaster or an energy bonanza with few ill effects—remains hotly debated.

"Old mines like the Orphan were mined in the 1950s under no federal regulations whatsoever," says Eugene Spiering, vice president of exploration for Quaterra. "Most mines today are above the water table, which makes chances of leakage practically nil. What we have now is a well-regulated industry."

Still, there has been no regionwide environmental assessment of the likely impact of a new uranium mining boom on the Colorado River, close observers say. Nor is such an evaluation apparently of much interest to federal land managers, if comments on the subject by a Department of Interior spokesman are any guide.

Uranium company officials say fears about radioactive contamination are overblown.

"We already have the Clean Water Act, the National Environmental Policy Act, and others that require comprehensive analyses before any mining is done, so there won't be impacts to the environment," says Chris Paolino, a spokesman for the Department of Interior. "At this time we're still evaluating plans on an individual basis, but [a regional study is] not something I can rule out."

An Impact Study Is Needed

"We hear from the industry and federal government that today 'we can do it safely,'" says Roger Clark, air and energy director for the Grand Canyon Trust, an environmental watchdog group. "But the burden of proof is on the proponents. Somebody needs to ask, 'What is the cumulative threat to drinking water in the Colorado River—not just from radioactivity, but from arsenic and mercury from these mines?'"

Some are asking for exactly such a study. With cities like Phoenix relying on clean Colorado River water, Arizona Gov. Janet Napolitano (D) is calling for an "overall environmental impact analysis," citing the uranium boom's "potential to seriously harm" the water quality of Grand Canyon National Park and the Lower Colorado River.

Uranium company officials say fears about radioactive contamination are overblown. New mining methods, far tougher environmental standards, and desert-dry conditions for most mines mean minimal risk to the Colorado River and the region's precious groundwater resources, they say.

Protection of water quality in the Colorado River is vital to the long-term health and safety of humans and other species.

"Yes, there were issues in the past," says Ron Hochstein, president of Denison Mines, a Toronto-based company with at least nine mines under development in the area targeted by Congress. "But that's not the way we do things today. We understand and know a lot more about uranium, radium, and radon and the impacts of those. So to say some things that happened in the 1950s and 1960s will happen again today is not a good comparison."

Proven Deposits Are Likely to Be Mined

Whether or not the thousands of unproven claims are ever developed, a fair number of uranium mining sites seem almost certain to reemerge. "Congress's action only applies to unproven claims," Mr. Clark points out, leaning against a fence at the Canyon Mine site.

Denison's group of established mine sites—including the Canyon Mine in the Kaibab National Forest a few miles south of the park—are among those likely to reemerge. The Canyon Mine was mothballed in the 1980s—before it had even opened—because of sinking uranium prices. It is a proven site: Uranium is there. Denison must still apply for new state environmental permits in order to proceed, but expects its mines to begin opening around 2010.

Despite Horn Creek pollution, the good news is that recent studies have shown that most springs and creeks in the Grand Canyon still have good water quality: Uranium and other trace metals appear in low concentrations, according to congressional testimony.

The bad news, experts say, is that digging into the cylindrical vertical rock formations in which uranium is found—they're called "breccia pipes"—can "mobilize" the uranium, causing it to oxidize when water from periodic downpours seeps down through the rock strata.

Indeed, the negative impact of water on uranium mines should not be minimized even in the desert, says Chris Shuey, a scientist who directs the Uranium Impact Assessment Program, a nonprofit research and information center. His research in the Churchrock area of the Navajo Nation near Gallup, N.M.—where uranium was mined and processed between 1952 and 1983—showed statistically significant effects on human health from the elevated levels of radioactivity in the region.

While much uranium in the region does occur in formations above the water table, the bottom of the breccia pipes are located in the upper portion of the Redwall Limestone, a principal aquifer supplying springs in the Grand Canyon and wells for much of the region, Dr. Shuey told Congress in March [2008].

Water Could Be Contaminated

"When you take uranium and the other trace elements out of their resting places in nature and expose them to the environment," Shuey says by phone, "you expose them in higher concentrations to the environment and intensify their effects. People don't appreciate the cumulative impact of mining in a consolidated area. There's a very real threat." A flash flood swept through Havasu Creek last week. That same watershed includes the Canyon Mine and numerous uranium claims.

Abe Springer, a hydrologist and researcher at Northern Arizona University at Flagstaff, has made a career studying the movement of groundwater through the Redwall and other aquifers into seeps and springs that supply not only hikers, but also most of the region's animal life with the water they need to survive.

"Once these elements became mobile through mining activities," Dr. Springer told Congress in his March testimony, "they would continue to be mobile through the aquifer and eventually discharge in springs impacting the human uses of water of these springs."

Even so, some industry figures dispute any connection between the Orphan uranium mine and higher radiation in Horn Creek.

A "fact sheet" e-mailed by Quaterra's Mr. Spiering says, regarding water pollution, that "statements that the historic operations at the Orphan Mine have been polluting Horn Creek are false." It cites a 2004 US Geological Survey [USGS] study showing dissolved uranium in a range from 8.6 to 29 parts per billion [p.p.b.] and "within the EPA [Environmental Protection Agency] levels of safe drinking water."

A Closer Look at the USGS Study

But a closer examination of the 2004 results finds that some uranium concentrations are at the upper end of the safe range for Horn Creek.

The same study's results for nearby Salt Creek (at 29 to 31 p.p.b.) "approached or exceeded the US Environmental Protection Agency's drinking water standard" of 30 p.p.b., according to Shuey's testimony to Congress.

The two creeks—Salt and Horn—also had by far the highest levels of the 20 springs and seeps tested in that study, Shuey testified. That USGS study also did not seek to assign causes of the higher radiation levels, he noted.

But the potential impact of tainted groundwater on native Americans, hikers, and local wildlife—as well as major cities downstream—are all reasons Rep. Rául Grijalva (D) of Arizona has sponsored legislation to permanently withdraw federal land around Grand Canyon National Park from uranium mining.

"I hope we've matured enough not to forget history," Representative Grijalva says in a phone interview. "Protection of water quality in the Colorado River is vital to the long-term health and safety of humans and other species. We can't afford to simply issue permits and decades from now simply dismiss the consequences as unintended.

"We should know better than that."

Editor's Note: As of July 2010, The Grand Canyon Watersheds Protection Act was still being considered by House of Representatives subcommittees.

10

Uranium Can Be Mined Sustainably

Heather Kent

Heather Kent is an environmental writer based in Vancouver, Canada.

The uranium mining industry has realized that operating in a sustainable way can be better for business. Rather than chafe against government regulations that require companies to report details about their mining practices, many companies are going beyond what is required in order to set new, higher standards for health, safety, and environmental practices in the industry. By gaining the trust of the public in this way, companies encounter less resistance to their projects and get more support from those who live near the mines. Being seen as responsible has paid off for uranium mining companies because good sustainability practices are good business; they help attract investors and employees and generate community support for mining operations.

Nuclear power is hot. Advocates of nuclear energy promote its low carbon cost as the way to reconcile surging global energy needs with the challenges of climate change. But something often gets lost in the discussion of the environmental superiority of nuclear energy over fossil fuels: questions about the sustainability of uranium mines.

According to the World Nuclear Organization's March 2008 statistics, China is constructing six nuclear reactors and

Heather Kent, "Sustainable Uranium Mining: Grappling with the New Realities," *Uranium Investing News*, May 24, 2008. Reproduced by permission.

has 86 more on the drawing board. In order to fuel these plants, China needs 1,396 tonnes of uranium this year, which is only slightly lower than Canada's requirements of 1,665 tonnes. India wants to more than double the number of its reactors and needs 978 tonnes of uranium to operate its existing 17 reactors. France will be using 10,527 tonnes of uranium in 2008 in its 59 nuclear reactors. Cameco Corporation, which accounts for 20% of world uranium production, estimates an increase in net generating capacity of about 21% by 2016.

Meanwhile, Dr. Gavin Mudd of the Institute for Sustainable Water Resources at Monash University in Victoria, Australia, argues that a significant amount of the GHG [greenhouse gas] emissions for nuclear power comes from uranium mining and milling. And that only limited information on emissions has been reported by mining companies.

First Analysis of Sustainability

Mudd's 2007 paper, "Sustainability Aspects of Uranium Mining: Towards Accurate Accounting," published in a recent issue of *Environmental Science and Technology*, was, he says, the first analysis of environmental sustainability in modern uranium mines. "There has never been an analysis that I have found that has used actual, reported data for different uranium mines," says Mudd. "It's always been assumed that the energy costs coming from the mining side are pretty low, relative to those coming from say the production of nuclear power. Also, people didn't realize that the data was available. Now that companies are releasing sustainability reports, a lot of that data is in there."

It is really only since 2000 that most companies have started to put numbers to things.

Western Mining Corporation (now BHP) was the first to issue sustainability reports in Australia in 1995 for its copper and uranium mining operations. "They were ahead of the whole mining industry globally on this," says Mudd, who has written extensively on the subject. Rio Tinto, which with BHP operates 90% of Australia's uranium mines, followed suit in 1997. Mudd credits Rio Tinto for providing site-specific environmental data, such as the effects of ore grade on energy costs, which he says should be the standard for all companies worldwide. (Rio Tinto did not respond to requests for an interview.)

BHP provides only a company-wide report. Mudd says, given the company's massive divisions, that's a real problem. "Before Rio Tinto, in the late 90s, a lot of reporting was mostly words from a lot of companies. It is really only since 2000 that most companies have started to put numbers to things" he says. "However, those numbers need to cover all aspects of operations. Some gold companies will give you the amount of cyanide they use, but they don't give you the amount of CO_2 [carbon dioxide] they release. And other companies will give you CO_2 figures but not water. When you want to try and really understand sustainability analyses from a strategic point of view about the direction that the industry needs to go in, you can't just use one figure for a whole company," says Mudd.

Larger Mines Bring Bigger Challenges

Some of the major environmental sustainability issues in Australian uranium mines are found in the expanded operations that have replaced small underground mines, Mudd says. "Now we are dealing with big, open-cast mines with a lot of waste rock and tailings to manage so the environmental costs are going up as grades go down." The large amount of trucking to process ore on-site is a significant producer of direct CO_2 emissions, he says.

Australia has large remaining uranium resources, which in itself poses challenges. "If you extrapolate forward 50 years, the mining companies will say they are going to continue increasing production. We need to know how much energy and therefore CO_2 emissions that will produce. If we look at the directions we are trying to achieve with climate change where we want 60% or 70% cuts in GHG emissions by 2050, we have to triple production on a lower grade resource which we know means a higher CO_2 cost per tonne of uranium and yet we still have to cut greenhouse emissions by 70%," says Mudd.

Sustainability measures cover communities, the environment and employee health and safety.

As far as underground uranium mining goes, depth is expected to emerge as a big issue. "We know from South Africa the amount of energy they have to use to go down sometimes two or three kilometers for their gold mines," says Mudd. At the same time he concedes that with the higher grade ore generally found in underground mining, the payback is also higher.

Measuring Sustainability

Cameco Corporation operates nine mines in Northern Saskatchewan, the US and Kazakhstan. Its sustainability measures cover communities, the environment and employee health and safety, says Gord Struthers, a company spokesman. "Having regulators looking over your shoulder," is a major driver on performance, he says. "Obviously, because we are dealing with uranium, we are subject to far closer regulatory scrutiny than other mining companies. Our goal is to get in front of regulatory compliance so that Cameco is actually defining the best practices," he says.

For example, the company is looking for new technology and systems to exceed the required targets for water treatment at its milling operations. One way in which the company reduces its environmental footprint is by transporting ore by road from the McArthur River and Cigar Lake mines to its milling sites rather than building new facilities and using more land. The company uses the ISO 14001 certification standard for environmental management, which involves a "plan-to-do" checklist approach to rectifying risks to the environment. Independent auditors carry out rigorous, annual site visits to ensure environmental management is effective, says Struthers.

Operating sustainably has definitely become the new way of attracting investors and doing business.

Social Responsibility

On the social sustainability front, Cameco has successfully worked with the primarily First Nations communities around their Northern Saskatchewan operations, says Struthers. Residents make up more than half of the workforce and the company helps local people develop their own businesses. In 2007, 71% of services contracted by Cameco were provided by businesses owned by northern residents.

Gaining social license in this way—community trust and support for uranium mining operations—is a growing aspect of sustainability. Joseph Ringwald, Vice-President of Sustainable Development at Tournigan Energy Ltd, a Vancouver-based exploration company developing two uranium properties in Eastern Slovakia, says it's critical to operate in the uranium sector with integrity and responsibility to the local community and shareholders. Ringwald, who as Vice-President of the Canadian Institute of Mining, was instrumental in making sustainability a major theme of two recent, national conferences, says sustainability is being raised at conferences and workshops more and more, but the industry is just beginning to understand that social license is the number one issue facing the global mining sector. "The major companies know this and there is a plethora of juniors who are beginning to understand this," he says. Still, operating sustainably has definitely become the new way of attracting investors and doing business. "Many investors are looking for companies that have good social performance and these are typically the majors. We need to learn from the majors that have fully engaged social license teams. Because they are so big, they can afford to hire sociologists, anthropologists and so on—in many cases before they send in exploration teams," says Ringwald.

Sustainability Is Good for Business

Cameco's Struthers agrees. "We are aware that sustainability is becoming an increasingly important factor in investment decisions that affect our business. You really have to walk the talk in this business." However, the cost of sustainability social licensing programs is a significant issue for the junior mining sector. It takes funding which is far more affordable for the major companies.

And despite the cost challenges for junior companies, Ringwald contends that when major companies come calling for acquisitions they are not only looking for technically strong projects, but also for the social licensing aspects that junior companies have developed with their affected communities. Many junior companies are only now beginning to realize this, he says. He also points out that some North and South American companies did not earn their social license to operate and "those projects are all gone now with the loss of hundreds of millions if not billions of dollars from the markets."

The global demand for uranium presents companies with a powerful opportunity to substantially improve their sustainability practices to attract investors, employees and community support for their operations. Business is changing in the ore patch.

11

The Supply of Uranium Is Adequate to Meet Demand

Nuclear Energy Institute

The Nuclear Energy Institute is the policy organization of the nuclear energy and technologies industry.

As the American uranium infrastructure grows along with the renewed demand for nuclear power, Russian uranium and other secondary sources will adequately supplement the domestic supply. Uranium-fueled nuclear power is much cheaper than coal, natural gas or oil, and even significant increases in the price of uranium will have little effect on the cost of nuclear-generated electricity. Industry analysts expect that there is enough uranium to meet current and future U.S. nuclear power needs, even as the demand for it grows.

In 2007, uranium of U.S. origin accounted for 8 percent of the material purchased by the owners and operators of U.S. nuclear power plants. The remainder (47 million pounds) came from foreign sources.

The U.S. uranium production industry is working to increase domestic supplies. For example, 2007 expenditures for

"Uranium Fuel Supply Adequate to Meet Present and Future Nuclear Energy Demand," *Nuclear Energy Institute*, 2009. Reproduced by permission. Some of the material summarized in this book is the property of the Nuclear Energy Institute (NEI). Copyright 2010 by NEI. That material has been summarized and included/reprinted here with permission from NEI. NEI does not warrant the accuracy or completeness of the summary of its material, and disclaims any and all liability stemming from any uses of or reliance upon the material. No NEI material may be copied or reprinted without NEI's permission.

uranium exploration in the United States were up 116 percent from 2006. Revitalization of the U.S. uranium production industry also brightens the job outlook. Although the industry remains comparatively small, employment rose 63 percent above the 2006 level.

One of the challenges facing the fuel supply sector—and their customers—is the long lead time to develop new mines and other fuel-cycle facilities. For example, a typical mine requires about 10 years of development before it begins producing commercially. Other challenges include localized opposition to mining, difficulties in hiring skilled employees, technical issues and market risk.

Other Sources of Uranium

In addition to traditional uranium deposits, the U.S. Department of Energy has a stockpile of uranium that it plans to release to the market over the next decade. This is just one of the "secondary sources" of uranium. Others include excess commercial inventories, the expected delivery of low-enriched uranium from Russian warheads, re-enrichment of depleted uranium tails (byproducts from enrichment operations), and possible reprocessing of used nuclear fuel.

Even with a significant increase in uranium price, nuclear energy has the lowest production costs.

Uranium also is available from non-conventional sources, such as the recovery of uranium byproduct from other metal mining (e.g., from copper mining in Utah), phosphate fertilizer mining (e.g., Florida, Morocco and Brazil) or gold mining (e.g., South Africa, where millions of tons of gold mining tailings are being processed for their uranium contents). As an example of the potential value of these sources, worldwide phosphate deposits contain about 22 million tons of uranium.

The United States Allows More Russian Uranium

In 2008, the United States and the Russian Federation amended the 1992 U.S./Russian Suspension Agreement that limited imports of Russian low-enriched uranium (LEU).

Even with further increases in the price of uranium, the cost of nuclear-generated electricity will remain low and competitive with other electricity sources.

The amended suspension agreement will give the Russian Federation limited access to the U.S. market starting in 2011 and extending through 2020. The agreement limits Russian exports to 16,559 kilograms of LEU in 2011 and gradually expands the limit to 514,754 kilograms in 2020. This is material beyond that available under the U.S./Russian High-Enriched Uranium Agreement. The U.S. Commerce Department will amend the limits as indicated based on changing demand projections.

Although the amended agreement retains limits on Russian LEU imports, it will increase the amount of uranium available to U.S. electric companies for nuclear plant fuel.

Fuel Is a Small Part of Nuclear Plant Production Cost

Even with a significant increase in uranium price, nuclear energy has the lowest production costs of any large-scale source of electricity, with the exception of hydroelectric power plants. In 2007, the production cost of nuclear-generated electricity was 1.76 cents per kilowatt-hour (kwh), compared with 2.47 cents per kwh for coal, 6.78 cents per kwh for natural gas and 10.26 cents for oil.

Nuclear fuel accounts for 27 percent of the overall production cost (fuel plus operations and maintenance expenses) of nuclear energy, versus 77 percent for coal and 92 percent for natural gas.

The cost of uranium (without processing) constitutes 35 percent of nuclear fuel. Nuclear fuel costs are not directly related to the spot price for uranium. The large increases in uranium prices over the past three years only increase the overall production cost of electricity generated at nuclear power plants by a few tenths of a cent per kilowatt-hour. Even with further increases in the price of uranium, the cost of nuclear-generated electricity will remain low and competitive with other electricity sources.

12

The False Clean Energy Promise Is a Front to Expand Uranium Mining

Jim Green

Jim Green is a national nuclear campaigner for Friends of the Earth, a community-based activist organization in Australia that works toward an ecologically sustainable and socially equitable society.

The promise of nuclear energy as a clean, green energy solution is a false promise, and it is not a solution to climate change. It is a front to promote the business interests that are involved in uranium mining. Australia exports its uranium to numerous other countries for a lucrative profit. However, in the long run the uranium industry is neither financially nor environmentally sustainable. The search for climate change solutions must not be an excuse to resuscitate the nuclear power industry.

The nuclear industry has once again tried to exploit concern about climate change to reverse its ongoing decline.

One positive aspect of this debate is that it has highlighted the need for action to avert the adverse social and environmental impacts associated with climate change. The debate has shifted—the science has been accepted and we are now debating solutions.

It is widely accepted that global greenhouse gas emissions must be reduced by at least 60% by the middle of the century

Jim Green, "Nuclear Power No Solution to Climate Change," September, 2005. Reproduced by permission of the author.

to stabilise atmospheric concentrations of greenhouse gases. We urgently need to change the way we produce and consume energy, and it is now clear that Australia and other countries cannot continue to rely on coal for electricity generation without major climate impacts.

Key environmental and medical groups reject nuclear power as a method at reducing greenhouse gas emissions. Nuclear power poses unacceptable proliferation and security risks, it is not clean, it is not cheap, and there is no solution to the intractable problem of nuclear waste.

Nuclear interests are far more concerned to expand uranium mining than to promote the introduction of nuclear power reactors.

The true climate-friendly solutions to Australia's energy and greenhouse problems lie in the fields of renewable energy—such as wind and solar power—and stopping energy wastage. This report shows that nuclear power is a dangerous and inefficient way to address climate change. It also shows why policy-makers should focus on the practical benefits provided by renewable energy and energy efficiency—safe, proven technologies available now.

Rekindling the Nuclear Debate

The nuclear industry, long in decline in Europe and the US, has seized on climate change to promote nuclear power as a 'climate friendly' energy source. However, there is little political support for the introduction of nuclear power in Australia.

Nuclear power is currently unlawful under the 1998 Australian Radiation Protection and Nuclear Safety Act, while Victoria and New South Wales also have legislation banning nuclear power and nuclear waste storage and disposal. Three other states—South Australia, Western Australia and the

Northern Territory—have legal prohibitions against various forms of radioactive waste transportation and dumping.

In Australia, nuclear interests are far more concerned to expand uranium mining rather than to promote the introduction of nuclear power reactors.

The current regulatory environment for uranium mining is inadequate.

The adverse environmental impacts of uranium mining in Australia have been significant. This year's [2005] prosecution of ERA (majority owned by Rio Tinto) over its operations at the Ranger uranium mine in the Northern Territory highlights the risks. The Olympic Dam uranium/copper mine in South Australia illustrates the scale of the environmental impacts associated with uranium mining. The Olympic Dam mine has produced a radioactive tailings dump of 60 million tonnes, growing at 10 million tonnes annually with no plans for its long-term management. The mine's daily extraction of over 30 million litres of water from the Great Artesian Basin has adversely impacted on the fragile Mound Springs, and the mine is a large consumer of electricity and a major contributor to South Australia's greenhouse gas emissions.

Inadequate Regulation

A further concern is that the current regulatory environment for uranium mining is inadequate. For example, the Olympic Dam mine enjoys a range of exemptions from the South Australian Environmental Protection Act, the Water Resources Act, the Aboriginal Heritage Act and the Freedom of Information Act.

The 2003 Senate Inquiry into the regulation of uranium mining in Australia reported "a pattern of under-performance and non-compliance", it identified "many gaps in knowledge and found an absence of reliable data on which to measure the extent of contamination or its impact on the environment", and it concluded that changes were necessary "in order to protect the environment and its inhabitants from serious or irreversible damage".

Attempts to establish new uranium mines would likely result in further examples of mining companies exerting unwanted pressure on Indigenous communities, as with the attempt to override the Mirarr traditional owners' unanimous opposition to the Jabiluka mine.

Australia's uranium mining industry may expand with proposed exports to China and India. Both China and India have nuclear weapons programs. India is not even a signatory to the Non Proliferation Treaty (NPT). China is not an open society and faces serious, unresolved human rights issues. It is difficult to imagine a nuclear industry worker in China publicly raising safety, security or proliferation concerns without reprisal.

Exports a Cause for Concern

Australia's uranium exports are already a cause for concern. Why do we allow uranium sales to Japan given the grossly inadequate safety culture in the nuclear industry there, as demonstrated by a number of serious and fatal accidents over the past decade and by revelations of systematic falsification of safety data? Why do we turn a blind eye to the regional tensions arising from Japan's plutonium program and its status as a 'threshold' or 'breakout' state capable of producing nuclear weapons in a short space of time?

Why do we allow uranium sales to South Korea when only last year [in 2004] it was revealed that numerous nuclear weapons research projects were secretly carried out there from the 1980s until 2000, in violation of the country's NPT obligations?

Why do we allow uranium sales to the US, the UK [United Kingdom] and France—nuclear weapons states which are failing to fulfil their NPT disarmament obligations? As retired Australian diplomat Richard Butler notes: "[The NPT] is a two-way—not one-way—street. It provides that states which do not have nuclear weapons must never acquire them and that those which do have them must progressively get rid of them." . . .

Most of the earth's uranium is found in very poor grade ores, and recovery of uranium from these ores is likely to be considerably more greenhouse intensive.

Nuclear Power Has Limited Potential

There are significant constraints on the growth of nuclear power, such as its high capital cost and, in many countries, lack of public acceptability. As a method of reducing greenhouse gas emissions, nuclear power is further limited because it is used almost exclusively for electricity generation, which is responsible for less than one third of global greenhouse gas emissions.

Because of these problems, the potential for nuclear power to help reduce greenhouse gas emissions by replacing fossil fuels is limited. Few predict a doubling of nuclear power output by 2050, but even if it did eventuate it would still only reduce greenhouse gas emissions by about 5%—less than one tenth of the reductions required to stabilise atmospheric concentrations of greenhouse gases.

Nuclear power is being promoted as the solution to climate change, as a technical fix or magic bullet. Clearly it is no such thing. As a senior analyst from the International Atomic Energy Agency, Alan McDonald, said in 2004: "Saying that nuclear power can solve global warming by itself is way over the top".

Nuclear power is not a 'renewable' energy source. High-grade, low-cost uranium ores are limited and will be exhausted in about 50 years at the current rate of consumption. The estimated total of all conventional uranium reserves is estimated to be sufficient for about 200 years at the current rate of consumption. But in a scenario of nuclear expansion, these reserves will be depleted more rapidly.

Nuclear Power Is Not Climate Friendly

Claims that nuclear power is 'greenhouse free' are incorrect as substantial greenhouse gas emissions are generated across the nuclear fuel cycle. Fossil-fuel generated electricity is more greenhouse intensive than nuclear power, but this comparative benefit will be eroded as higher-grade uranium ores are depleted. Most of the earth's uranium is found in very poor grade ores, and recovery of uranium from these ores is likely to be considerably more greenhouse intensive.

Nuclear power emits more greenhouse gases per unit [of] energy than most renewable energy sources, and that comparative deficit will widen as uranium ore grades decline.

Organizations to Contact

The editors have compiled the following list of organizations concerned with the issues debated in this book. The descriptions are derived from materials provided by the organizations. All have publications or information available for interested readers. The list was compiled on the date of publication of the present volume; the information provided here may change. Readers need to remember that many organizations take several weeks or longer to respond to inquiries.

Beyond Nuclear

6930 Carroll Ave., Suite 400, Takoma Park, MD 20912
(301) 270-2209 • fax: (301) 270-4000
e-mail: info@beyondnuclear.org
Web site: www.beyondnuclear.org

Beyond Nuclear works to educate the public about the connections between nuclear power and nuclear weapons and the need to abandon both to safeguard the future of humanity. Beyond Nuclear advocates for an energy future that is sustainable, benign, and democratic. The organization publishes a quarterly newsletter, *The Thunderbird*, which often contains articles about uranium mining and related issues. The Beyond Nuclear Web site includes an archive of news articles about uranium mining and processing as well as useful uranium-related material that can be downloaded, such as the brochure, "Uranium Mining and Human Rights."

Indigenous Environmental Network (IEN)

PO Box 485, Bemidji, MN 56619
(218) 751-4967
e-mail: martyc@ienearth.org
Web site: www.ienearth.org

Established in 1990, the Indigenous Environmental Network was formed by grassroots indigenous peoples to address environmental and economic justice issues, including toxic and radioactive pollution from uranium mining on indigenous lands. Its "Mineral Extraction on Indigenous Lands" project online includes a wealth of resources for students and activists alike. Streaming videos on the IEN Web site include the music video titled "Amerika" and the two-part anti-mining documentary "Vanishing Prayer—Native American Grandmothers at Big Mountain Resist Relocation."

Nuclear Energy Institute (NEI)
1776 I St. NW, Suite 400, Washington, DC   20006-3708
(202) 739-8000 • fax: (202) 785-4019
e-mail: info@nei.org
Web site: www.nei.org

The Nuclear Energy Institute is the policy organization of the nuclear energy and technologies industry. It participates in both the national and global policy-making process. NEI produces a monthly newsletter, *Nuclear Energy Insight*, as well as many other publications. Its Web site includes an archive of statistical data pertaining to uranium mining and the nuclear energy industry, as well as transcripts of Congressional testimony relating to the same. NEI's large collection of reports, brochures, graphics, and other materials can be browsed online.

Nuclear Information and Resource Service (NIRS)
6930 Carroll Ave., Suite 340, Takoma Park, MD   20912
(301) 270-6477 • fax: (301) 270-4291
e-mail: nirsnet@nirs.org
Web site: www.nirs.org

NIRS is an information and networking center for people and organizations concerned about nuclear power, radioactive waste, radiation, and sustainable energy issues. NIRS initiates large-scale organizing and public education campaigns on specific issues, such as preventing construction of new nuclear reactors or halting the development of uranium mines. In conjunction with the World Information Service on Energy, NIRS publishes the international newsletter, *WISE/NIRS*

Nuclear Monitor, twenty times a year in both English and Spanish. The NIRS Web site offers a variety of news articles and reports about uranium mining and milling, both domestic and international. Numerous fact sheets are available online including, "America's Secret Chernobyl—Uranium Mining and Nuclear Pollution in the Upper Midwest," and "Nuclear Power—the Next De-Generation."

U.S. Department of Energy (DOE)
1000 Independence Ave. SW, Washington, DC   20585
(202) 586-5000 • fax: (202) 586-4403
e-mail: The.Secretary@hq.doe.gov
Web site: www.energy.gov

The U.S. Department of Energy takes control of abandoned uranium mines and closed and reclaimed mills, as authorized by Congress. Its Web site archives nearly 12,000 documents related to uranium and uranium mining, including such things as environmental impact reports, fact sheets, studies, official findings and testimony, and statements of various kinds. All of the files can be searched and accessed from the DOE Web site, making it an excellent resource for finding out the regulatory history of a specific mine.

U.S. Environmental Protection Agency (EPA)
Ariel Rios Building. 1200 Pennsylvania Ave. NW
Washington, DC   20460
(202) 272-0167
e-mail: radiation.questions@epa.gov
Web site: www.epa.gov

The U.S. Environmental Protection Agency is the federal government agency charged with protecting human health and the environment by developing and enforcing regulations based on laws passed by Congress. The EPA sets environmental protection standards for uranium mining and milling and for handling uranium-based products. Its Web site offers informational fact sheets about uranium, uranium mining and uranium tailings, milling, and uses. Through the site's "RAD-

Town USA" project, visitors can explore a virtual community showing a wide variety of radiation sources and uses as people may encounter them in everyday life.

U.S. Nuclear Regulatory Commission (NRC)

11555 Rockville Pike, Rockville, MD   20852
(800) 368-5642 or (301) 415-7000
Web site: www.nrc.gov

The Nuclear Regulatory Commission is the government agency whose mission is to regulate the nation's civilian use of nuclear materials (including uranium) to ensure public health and safety and to protect the environment. The NRC licenses and oversees the operations of uranium mines and mills. The NRC Web site offers numerous brochures and fact sheets about uranium mining and nuclear power in general, and it maintains extensive document collections that include a wide array of congressional and commission transcripts, government reports and public documents specific to the rulemaking and enforcement functions of the agency.

Uranium Watch

PO Box 344, Moab, Utah   84532
(435) 210-0166
e-mail: info@uraniumwatch.org
Web site: www.uraniumwatch.org

Uranium Watch is a Utah-based nonprofit that advocates for protection of public health and the environment from past, current, and future impacts of uranium mining and milling and nuclear waste disposal at uranium mill sites. Uranium Watch publishes a monthly online newsletter, *Utah Bulletin*, which reports the latest uranium-related news. The organization's Web site offers a wide variety of news, information, and resources about current and historic uranium mining and milling activities and issues. The site is indispensable as an information clearinghouse because it maintains hundreds of links to the uranium-specific Web sites of governmental agencies, community groups, and mining industry organizations and companies.

World Information Service on Energy (WISE)
Uranium Project

Am Schwedenteich 4, 01477, Arnsdorf
  Germany
e-mail: uranium@t-online.de
Web site: www.wise-uranium.org

The World Information Service on Energy is an information and networking center for citizens and environmental organizations concerned about nuclear energy, radioactive waste, radiation, and related issues. WISE publishes the international newsletter, *WISE/NIRS Nuclear Monitor*, twenty times a year in both English and Spanish. The WISE Uranium Project specifically focuses on the health and environmental impacts of nuclear fuel production: uranium radiation and health effects, uranium mining and milling, enrichment and fuel fabrication, and depleted uranium. The WISE Uranium Project Web site maintains a comprehensive archive of news articles related to uranium mining, milling and enrichment, and it provides action alerts and other resources for anti-uranium activists. A series of informative "Slide Talks" that explore various aspects of uranium mining and nuclear fuel production can be viewed on the Web site.

World Nuclear Association (WNA)

22a St. James's Square, London   SW1Y 4JH
  United Kingdom
+44 (0)20 7451 1520 • fax: +44 (0)20 7839 1501
e-mail: wna@world-nuclear.org
Web site: www.world-nuclear.org

Formerly known as "The Uranium Institute," the World Nuclear Association is a global organization that seeks to promote the peaceful worldwide use of nuclear power as a sustainable energy resource for the future. Specifically, the WNA is concerned with nuclear power generation and all aspects of the nuclear fuel cycle, including uranium mining. The WNA Web site contains extensive information about nuclear fuel best practices, position statements and articles such as "Can

Uranium Supplies Sustain the Global Nuclear Renaissance?" An informative "Pocket Guide to Uranium" can be downloaded from the site.

Bibliography

Books

Michael Amundson	*Yellowcake Towns—Uranium Mining Communities in the American West.* Denver: University Press of Colorado, 2004.
Doug Brugge	*Memories Come to Us in the Rain and the Wind: Oral Histories and Photographs of Navajo Uranium Miners and Their Families.* Boston: The Navajo Uranium Miner Oral History and Photography Project, 1997.
Doug Brugge, Timothy Benally, and Esther Yazzie-Lewis	*The Navajo People and Uranium Mining.* Albuquerque, NM: University of New Mexico Press, 2007.
Gwyneth Cravens	*Power to Save the World: The Truth About Nuclear Energy.* New York: Vintage, reprint edition 2008.
Peter H. Eichstaedt	*If You Poison Us: Uranium and Native Americans.* Santa Fe, NM: Red Crane Books, 1994.
Malcolm Grimston and Peter Beck	*Double or Quits? The Future of Civil Nuclear Energy.* London: Earthscan, 2002.

Broder J. Merkel and Andrea Hasche-Berger — *Uranium in the Environment: Mining Impact and Consequences*. Berlin, Germany: Heidelberg Press, 2006.

Eric Mogren — *Warm Sands: Uranium Mill Tailings Policy in the Atomic West*. Santa Fe, NM: University of New Mexico Press, 2002.

Bindu Panikkar and Doug Brugge — *The Ethical Issues in Uranium Mining Research in the Navajo Nation*. New York: Taylor & Francis, 2007.

Raye Carleson Ringholz — *Uranium Frenzy: Saga of the Nuclear West*. Logan, UT: Utah State University Press, 2002.

Brice Smith — *Insurmountable Risks: The Dangers of Using Nuclear Power to Combat Global Climate Change*. Muskegon, MI: RDR Books and the Institute for Energy and Environmental Research Press, 2006.

William Tucker — *Terrestrial Energy: How Nuclear Energy Will Lead the Green Revolution and End America's Energy Odyssey*. Savage, MD: Bartleby Press, 2008.

Tom Zoellner — *Uranium: War, Energy and the Rock That Shaped the World*. New York: Viking Adult, 2009.

Periodicals

Ben Arnoldy — "Mining Revival: A Uranium Boom for a Wary West," *The Christian Science Monitor*, June 19, 2007.

Felicity Barringer "Uranium Exploration Near Grand Canyon," *New York Times*, February 7, 2008.

Rex Bowman "In Virginia, the Appeal of Uranium Mining," *TIME*, February 23, 2009.

Doug Brugge and Rob Goble "The History of Uranium Mining and the Navajo People," *American Journal of Public Health*, vol. 92, no. 9, 2002.

Dan Frosch "Uranium Mining Haunts Navajo Country," *New York Times*, July 26, 2009.

Anita Kumar "House Panel Rejects Study of Uranium Mining," *Washington Post*, March 4, 2008.

Jim Moscou "Uranium Heats Up," *Newsweek*, April 10, 2007.

Judy Pasternak "Blighted Homeland: The Series, Part 1. A Peril That Dwelt Among the Navajo," *Los Angeles Times*, November 19, 2006.

——— "Blighted Homeland: The Series, Part 2. Oases in Navajo Desert Contained 'A Witch's Brew,'" *Los Angeles Times*, November 20, 2006.

——— "Blighted Homeland: The Series, Part 3. Navajos' Desert Cleanup No More Than a Mirage," *Los Angeles Times*, November 21, 2006.

————   "Blighted Homeland: The Series, Part
               4. Mining Firms Again Eyeing Navajo
               Land," *Los Angeles Times*, November
               22, 2006.

James Peach and   "The Economic Impact of Proposed
Anthony Popp   Uranium Mining and Milling
                  Operations in the State of New
                  Mexico," Office of Policy Analysis,
                  Arrowhead Center, New Mexico State
                  University, August 1, 2008.

Stefan   "Blue People, Yellowcake," *In These
Simanowitz   Times*, March 4, 2009.

Shaun Burnie and "Japan's Nuclear Twilight Zone,"
Aileen Mioko   *Bulletin of the Atomic Scientists*,
Smith   May/June 2001.

Shelley Smithson "Radioactive Revival in New Mexico,"
                  The Nation, June 29, 2009.

Taylor Wiles   "Navajo Yellowcake Woes
                 Continue—When the EPA Evacuates
                 Your Town for Superfund Cleanup,
                 What Happens to the People Left
                 Behind?" *Mother Jones*, September 30,
                 2009.

Index

H

Havasupai Indians, 29–30
Health risks of uranium mining,
21–22
Horn, Rick Van, 59
Horwitt, Dusty, 64–71
House, Ben, 58
House Natural Resources Com-
mittee (U.S.), 74
HRI Energy (Texas), 58
Human Rights China (New York),
36
Hydrogen bonus (in U.S.), 47

I

In-situ leaching (ISL), 9–10, 17,
18, 19
   described, 40
   near national parks, 69
   water safety and, 32–33
Indall, John, 57
India
   aborigine anti-mining activities, 24–25
   nuclear energy expansion, 14,
47–48, 93
Indigenous people, exploitation of,
24–38
   Australian aborigines, 24–25
   call for global mining ban, 38
   legislation, 8, 26, 28
   Navajo Nation, 7–9, 22, 24–26
   Pueblo Indians, 22, 27, 28
Indigenous World Uranium Summit (2006), 24–25
Innuits of Nunavut, 46–47, 48,
53–54
International Physicians for the
Prevention of Nuclear War, 35

Inuit Circumpolar Conference,
52–53
Italy, nuclear energy expansion, 48

J

Jackpile Mine, 28
Jantz, Eric, 61

K

Kaibab National Forest (Arizona),
77
Kazakhstan, uranium supply data,
9, 13, 16
Kent, Heather, 80–85
Kiggavik-Sisson uranium deposit,
50
Kneen, Jamie, 33–34
Kucinich, Dennis, 9

L

LaDuke, Winona, 35
Laguna Pueblo Indians, 28
Lanzhou Prison (China), 38
Liquid radioactive uranium, 10
Loris, Nick, 12–19
Low-enriched uranium (LEU)
from Russia, 88

M

McCain, John, 51
McKinnon, Taylor, 75
Menominee Indian Nation
(Wisconsin), 23
Milling process
   agency regulation of, 41
   described, 17–19, 41, 48–49
   economics of, 47

Nuclear Regulatory Commission (NRC), 18, 41, 42–43, 51, 57, 69
Nuclear renaissance, 48–49
Nuclear testing, 30
Nuclear waste/waste dumps, 22–23, 27, 41
   See also Yucca Mountain disposal site

O

Obama, Barack, 10, 51
Off-shore natural gas, 12, 15
Olympic Dam uranium/copper mine, 92
Open pit mining, 8, 16–17, 40
Orphan uranium mine, 72–73, 78

P

Pino, Manuel, 28–29
Politics and nuclear power plants, 51–52
Pueblo Indians, 22, 27, 28

Q

Quaterra Resources mining company, 67–68, 74, 78

R

Radiation Exposure Compensation Act (1990), 8, 26, 36
Radioactive particles, 18, 28, 39, 72
Regulation of mining, 75
Russia-U.S. High Enriched Uranium Agreement, 88

S

Safety factors, in mining, 13, 18–19, 39–45

Salaries from mining, 56
Scheffler, Wolfgang, 36
Serpent River watershed (Canada), 33
Seventh Generation Fund, 35
Shirley, Joe, Jr., 22, 26, 31, 58
Shuey, Chris, 77
Soil radiation, 72
South Africa, uranium supply data, 13
South Australian Environmental Protection Act, 92
Southwest Information and Information Center, 32
Spencer, Jack, 12–19
Spiering, Eugene, 75
Springer, Abe, 78
Sustainable mining of uranium, 80–85

T

Tailings (mining waste)
   abandonment of, 8
   agency regulation of, 42–44
   described, 18–19, 41, 42, 59
   disposal issues, 21
   indiscriminate dumping of, 33
   Olympic Dam (Australia), 92
   South African gold mines, 87
Technologically-enhanced naturally occurring radioactive materials (TENORM), 40–41
Three Mile Island nuclear reactor accident, 57–58
Till, William von, 57
Tolousi, Carletta, 29